Curious Customs

Curious Customs

Customs

The Stories Behind 296 Popular American Rituals

TAD TULEJA

A Stonesong Press Book

Harmony Books/New York

Published by Harmony Books, a division of Crown Publishers, Inc., 225 Park Avenue South, New York, New York 10003 and represented in Canada by the Canadian MANDA Group

HARMONY and colophon are trademarks of Crown Publishers, Inc.

Manufactured in the United States of America

A Stonesong Press Book

Library of Congress Cataloging-in-Publication Data

Tuleja, Tad, 1944-
    Curious customs.

    "A Stonesong Press book."
    1. United States—Social life and customs.
2. Folklore—United States. I. Title.
E161.T84   1987   390'.0973   87-4098
ISBN 0-517-56653-2
    0-517-56654-0 (pbk.)

10 9 8 7 6 5 4 3 2 1

First Edition

CONTENTS

*For the folks I learned
these ways with:
Eddie, Betty Anne, and Greg*

INTRODUCTION

Suppose you're a visiting extraterrestrial, your spaceship lands somewhere in the vicinity of Chicago, and for several months, suitably
disguised, you are able to observe the inhabitants as they go about
their daily activities. At the end of this period, you return to your
home star and report to your superiors. If you applied to the Chicago
population the descriptive principles of terrestrial anthropologists,
you might include these observations:

On the typical formal costume: "Before all major social and commercial events, the males drape lengths of patterned cloth around
their necks, knotting them at the throat in a traditional triangular
design. The ends of this knotted cloth device are left to dangle on the
wearer's chest or, in certain clans, are fastened with a clip. No serious
business may be transacted until the participants have donned this
ceremonial attire."

On gift-giving: "Presents exchanged on festive occasions are
wrapped in decorative paper and are often further decorated with
ribbons before the honored individual receives them. Although great
care is taken with the wrapping, as soon as the present is opened, the
wrapping is disposed of as garbage."

On intoxicants: "The day begins with the drinking of hot stimulants and ends with the ingestion of cold depressants. The morning
'coffee ritual' is frequently private, the afternoon 'cocktail ceremony'
generally communal. Also, in spite of the governing council's attempts to suppress the practice, many Chicagoans burn leaves con-
taining a narcotic substance and inhale the smoke into their lungs."

If you were on the extraterrestrial governing council, what would
you make of our supposedly practical and reasonable social customs?

What can be said about a culture where women are expected to
remove the hair from under their arms, where virgins congregate to
catch fertility bouquets from newly married brides, where the winter

solstice festival includes the formal placement of large trees inside the natives' homes, and where the national anthem is most often heard at a ceremonial pastime that involves hitting a ball with a stick?

Curious Customs attempts to answer these and related questions about why we behave the way we do. It is a survey of the many socially sanctioned rituals and folkways that Americans take for granted but that no extraterrestrial ever could. Some of these are the "heavy" rituals of religion and superstition, but most are not. My principal concern is with the more mundane, "trivial" customs of daily life: activities associated with food, drink, costume, appearance, entertainment, work, and romance. The rituals, in other words, of where we live. In a whimsical, but I trust also a provocative, way, *Curious Customs* is a kind of *catalogue déraisonné* of everyday American life.

Where possible, the entries include information, or at least informed speculation, on the reasons behind our social ways: Wherever I can, I try to demonstrate the integrating functions of our *mores*. Where the social rationale for a given custom is not clear, I settle for describing its origin and leave it to the discerning reader to say whether or not it makes sense.

I do not offer the book as criticism, but as observation. If *Curious Customs* has a debunking bias, it is not a revolutionary one, for I do not suppose it makes any more sense for a businessman to stop wearing a tie than it does for him to continue wearing one. What does make sense is understanding the whens and wheres and whys of tie-wearing. The anthropologist's business here is to make it possible, as Socrates advised, for you, the reader, to "know yourself." What you do with the knowledge is your business.

Source citations in the text consist only of authors' names, with full citations in the Bibliography. (A date is used only when more than one work of an author is cited. Note also that the standard references that I used—a variety of dictionaries and encyclopedias—are listed by author and title in the headnote to the Bibliography.) For sending me information that was not publicly available, I am grateful to the Association of Bridal Consultants, the Eno Foundation, the Flag Research Center, the Gemological Institute of America, the H. J. Heinz Company, William Marvey, Montgomery Ward & Company, the Museum of Florida History, the National Baseball

Hall of Fame and Museum, the Oscar Mayer Company, the Pan-American Coffee Bureau, the Popcorn Institute, the Wm. Wrigley Jr. Company, and the Chambers of Commerce of St. Louis, Missouri, and Saratoga, New York. My appreciation also goes to the reference librarians at Amherst College and the University of Massachusetts and to the members of the university's anthroplogy department for their generous assistance; I want to particularly thank George Armelagos, who gave me good counsel on food entries, and Brooke Thomas, whose course on biocultural processes of change provided a stimulating introduction to the field. And a special thanks to my family, for enduring me while this monster was caged.

T.F.T.

Belchertown, Massachusetts
1987

In my country there is a belief—and rightly so—
that the only thing separating us from the animals
is mindless superstitions and pointless rituals.

—Latka in *Taxi*

What custom wills, in all things should we do't.

—*Coriolanus,* II, 3

Curious Customs

THAT'S THE TICKET:

ETIQUETTE

ETIQUETTE MANUALS

Rules for behavior are as old as civilization (the Egyptians had them in 2500 B.C.), but typically etiquette becomes a pressing matter only during periods of class instability. The first spate of European "conduct books" arose in the French and Italian Renaissance, during the twilight of feudalism and the rise of an urban merchant class. Social manners at this time became increasingly refined, as a way of keeping distance between the classes. Not surprisingly, the same impulse was at work during America's heyday of "usage" manuals, the commercial renaissance of the Gilded Age. According to Arthur Schlesinger, etiquette authorities now saw as their mission "to instill a more aristocratic style of behavior, one consonant with the improving fortunes of the middle class." Throughout Western history, therefore, etiquette has never strayed far from its original intent: to protect rulers from contact with "lesser persons."

The word itself is Old French for "ticket," meaning a written order indicating to a soldier where he was to be billeted. Military housing assignments, thus, may have been the first rules of etiquette. Eventually all orders of the day might have found their way onto large *etiquettes* posted conspicuously around army camps. Many authorities believe that such public lists of "things to be done" were the forerunners of etiquette manuals.

GREETINGS

Many greetings focus either on the general trend of events (the German *Wie geht's?,* the French *Comment ça va?,* the Mexican *Que pasa?,* the American *How's it going?* and *What's happening?*) or, even more directly, on the ontological status of the greetee (the Spanish *Como está?* and the English *How are you?*). Anglo-Americans have added an economic formula to this repertoire. The common query "How do you do?" is very likely a variant of "What do you do?"—the latter widely used by strangers who are sizing up each other's potential as business associates. In whatever form we meet it, the question suggests the pragmatic nature of American society and the distance our social classes have placed between their etiquette and that of the Old World.

What a European means, or at least used to mean, by the greeting "How are you?" was not so much "How?" as "Who?" In other words, "Who are your father and mother? What is your breeding line?" In America such questions are rarely asked. One asks initially "What do you do?" or "How do you do?" because it is generally understood that, with few exceptions, you will not prosper here without labor.

"EXCUSE ME"/"PARDON ME"

The two commonest apologies in our culture harken back to medieval prototypes. Although they are often used assertively—as when someone elbows his way through a crowd muttering, "Excuse me, I'm just going back to my seat"—linguistically both are clearly passive: They are announcements that one has transgressed a boundary and must beg forgiveness. The original transgressed boundaries were legal ones, and the formulas were the creation of canon and feudal law.

In the thirteenth century to "excuse" oneself meant to ask a magistrate literally to "remove the cause," that is, to absolve the person of responsibility in a legal proceeding. To beg for "pardon" meant much the same thing, with an added ecclesiastical weight: To be pardoned by the church meant that one's celestial as well as mundane dues had been lightened. In the fourteenth century, a pardoner was a wandering papal envoy licensed to sell pardons, or "indulgences."

FAREWELLS

The story of English farewells is one of increasing secularization. In the Middle Ages, people parted by saying "God be with you," a characteristically pious comment that had its parallels in the Spanish *adios* and the French *adieu.* However, the English form lost its blatant godliness, and as early as Shakespeare's time was coming out as "God bye." "Good bye" is a distortion of the early nineteenth century. That century also gave us the alternate "So long," that chummier leavetaking that has been linked to the Arabic *salaam* and the Hebrew *shalom,* but that is more likely derived from the German *solange,* "until that time" that we meet again. In its anticipation of a reunion, then, "so long" suggests both the more formal German *Aufwiedersehen* and its French equivalent *au revoir,* both of which mean "until we see each other again." The final step in the degeneration of partings took place in acid-blasted California, where late-1960s young people, too hip to believe in God and too now-oriented to even consider tomorrow, came up with the antiseptic "Have a nice day." That this vapid prayer became endemic may say as much about the hedonism and anomie of the 1970s as about the contagiousness of slang. One anxiously awaits the compression of this parting into "Handy."

LADIES FIRST

The forms of deference to the "weaker sex" that social custom enshrines are variants of a metaform that one might call the "pedestal ploy." The apparent function of the pedestal ploy is to proclaim the moral superiority of women by giving them benefits once reserved for royalty: giving up one's seat, opening doors, pulling out chairs, and rising when a woman enters the room. The ploy's hidden agenda is quite different. Over the centuries such pleasantries have infantilized women, kept them in their "higher" place, and maintained the convenient (for men) social fiction that females cannot perform real labor, and so need not be paid adequately for the labor they do perform. If the "little woman" can't open a door for herself, it's certainly not necessary to make her salary more than 60 percent of a man's.

This effect of the pedestal ploy was not, of course, always obvious. In the days when the ploy was used most widely, the females to whom these social courtesies were extended did not, in fact, know how to work: As the daughters of wealth, their function was to manage the conspicuous fortunes their husbands earned. Women who worked were by definition members of the "lower" orders, and being lower carried moral as well as social connotations. It is not an accident that the expression "working girl," which today means a professional prostitute, recently meant any woman with a job.

BOWING

The bow, like the curtsy, is out of fashion today since so few of us ever meet royalty. Most of us witness true bowing—rather than the curt head nod, its democratic descendant—only in theaters and night clubs. There is a subtle logic to this, for the bow that one gave a prince in former days and the bow that a performer gives today are at root the same gesture. Both reflect the ancient (indeed, biological) movement of lowering the head before a superior to signify respect, service, or obedience. The message of the bow is "You are greater than I am; please treat me well." Since rock stars, from "King" Elvis to today's Prince, make real princes look impoverished, it may seem inappropriate for performers to bend at the waist to royal viewers —or to the modern equivalent, their Majesties, the Mob. But the custom developed in simpler times, when a performer had considerably less social standing. Tradition has sustained the performer's bow even though that standing has risen dramatically. Strictly from the point of view of status, though, Michael Jackson probably should be receiving, not giving, the bows.

TIPPING ONE'S HAT

Few Americans tip their hats today, partly because etiquette has loosened and partly because they don't wear hats. Until the 1950s, however, men commonly tipped their hats to women, and removed them entirely in elevators. In doing so, they were carrying on a tradition that has its roots in Roman times. In ancient Rome a head covering was an emblem of social or political superiority. Sabine Baring-Gould observed that Julius Caesar was murdered because he had accepted "the merest shred of symbol," a royal headband, implying "that all save he were vassals and serfs." The sign of a freed slave, Baring-Gould also noted, was the so-called Phrygian cap, a floppy Near Eastern import that well into the nineteenth century still symbolized freedom.

Just as covering the head symbolized dominance, so uncovering it symbolized submission. Ever since the early Middle Ages, to remove one's hat—be it made of cloth or metal—has signified subservience to a superior. As an animal bares its throat or belly to a dominant rival, the feudal vassal bared his head to his lord, saying, in effect, "I am at your service; do with me as you will." This original sense of the ritual is mirrored in the expressions "with hat in hand" and "I take my hat off to him."

THE MILITARY SALUTE

Leopold Wagner's fanciful idea of the origin of the military salute is that it dates from medieval tournaments, when knights addressed the queen in this manner to shield their eyes from her blinding beauty. A less chivalrous, but more credible, explanation is that in the age of visored and armored horsemen, raising the visor was a signal between two knights that they meant each other no harm: The gesture provided recognition and with it the promise of amity.

THE MAN WALKS ON THE OUTSIDE

When a man and a woman walk together, convention says the man takes the curb side. A common historical explanation of this custom is that in the days when garbage was hurled into the street from upper-story windows, it was the man's duty to bear the majority of the refuse. More reasonable is the explanation that a man on the outside is in a better position to protect his female companion from the hazards of the street itself, which until fairly recently included runaway horses and street brawlers. Though Emily Post dutifully approved the custom she denied its usefulness in the days of automobiles. Apparently she had never negotiated a New York City sidewalk just after a downpour.

SMALL TALK

The distinctive characteristic of small talk is that it is noncontroversial. The art of conversation is literally that of "turning things over together," but small talk does nothing of the kind. Light, polite conversation is the oral embodiment of Emily Post's "first rule for behavior in company": "Try to do and say only that which will be agreeable to others."

Ironically this bland mode of discourse came to fruition when public education was on the rise. Horace Mann's legacy ought to have been more, not less, intellectual exchange, but this seems not to have been the case. Mass learning in the nineteenth century resulted, not in an educated populace eager to turn over new ideas, but merely in an *informed* populace, victims of the adage that a little learning is a dangerous thing and fiercely proud of the democratic fiction that everyone's opinion has equal merit. Small talk became popular as a corrective, and was popularized chiefly by social arbiters, who understood it, quite rightly, as a way of keeping the opinionated at bay. Thus a great, unrecognized consequence of the Gilded Age's etiquette mania was to silence real social inquiry by making it impolite to discuss such controversial topics as politics at table.

BUSINESS CARDS

Today business cards are distributed with abandon by working people of all social classes, illustrating not only the ubiquity of commercial interests but also the fluidity of the world of trade. Whether one is buttonholing potential clients for a carpentry service, announcing one's latest academic appointment, or "networking" with fellow executives, it is permissible to advertise one's talents and availability by an outstretched hand and the statement "Here's my card." As Robert Louis Stevenson once observed, everybody makes his living by selling *something*. Business cards facilitate this endeavor.

It has not always been this way. The cards that we use today for commercial purposes are a vulgarization of the nineteenth-century social calling card, an artifact with a quite different purpose. In the Gilded Age, possessing a calling card indicated not that you were interested in forming business relationships, but that your money was so old (or so you wanted people to think) that you had no need to make a living. For the calling-card class, life was a continual round of social visits, and the protocol governing these visits was inextricably linked to the proper use of cards. Pick up any etiquette manual predating World War I, and you will find whole chapters devoted to such questions as whether a single gentleman may leave a card for a lady; when a lady must, and must not, turn down the edges of a card; and whether an unmarried girl of between fourteen and seventeen may carry more than six or less than thirteen cards in her purse in months beginning with a "J." The calling card system was especially cherished by those who made no distinction between manners and mere form, and its preciousness was well defined by that doyenne of the dim, Mrs. John Sherwood. Her 1887 manual called the card "the field mark and device" of civilization.

The business version of the calling card came in around the turn of the century, when the formerly well defined borders between the commercial and the personal realms were beginning to blur. In the decades when both types of cards still were used widely, society mavens considered it unforgivable to fuse the two realms. Emily Post's contemporary Lillian Eichler called it very poor taste to use business cards for social purposes, and as late as 1967 Amy Vanderbilt counseled that the merchant's marker "may never double for social purposes."

URINAL ETIQUETTE

The privatization of public urination is a relatively recent phenomenon. Originally urinals were simply common troughs, set either slightly below waist level or into the floor. Separate urinals came in only in the 1940s, and the dividers between them did not come in until the 1950s. Dale Guthrie has argued that this movement toward isolation while pissing is a structural response to increasing congestion. Congestion creates stress, which can be relieved temporarily by urination. Thus a person having a trying day at work goes to the bathroom more frequently. But these trips indicate as well as release tension, so that frequent bladder-emptying is a signal to others that one is agitated.

Urinals now being separated from each other may represent a vestigial puritan distaste for one's "privates," but interurinal barriers may also provide artificial, almost theatrical, screens between pissers, symbolically shielding them from the discomfort associated with invaded space. The social dynamics of the male bathroom, of course, forbid one to look over or around these barriers or, when there are no barriers, to look left or right at all. This is not so much because of the sexual threat implied but because such intrusion breaches the unspoken code that unites pissers in a denial of their vulnerability.

ELEVATOR BEHAVIOR

What's the worst thing that can happen to you in an elevator? Mugging? Falling twenty floors to your death? Terrifying possibilities, but pale in comparison with what I believe to be every elevator rider's secret phobia: being stuck between floors, perhaps forever. Because of this fear, we have evolved precise, if unwritten, rules for behaving in an elevator. You must not speak to other passengers (except for quickly mumbled hellos), you must not establish eye contact, and you must face the door. This establishes an extreme impersonality, even a kind of invisibility, and this is precisely the attitude to have in a situation from which you cannot wait to be rescued. Establishing a relationship in an elevator would be tantamount to admitting that the fearful vehicle in which you are suspended is not a temporary aberration but perhaps a temporary home. Structurally an elevator car resembles both a jail cell and a burial vault; in order to deny these resemblances, we make ourselves deaf, dumb, and blind.

IN THE WINK OF AN EYE:

GESTURES AND POSTURES

SHAKING HANDS

Handshaking is used to greet another and to "seal" a contract or a promise. The joining of hands at a wedding represents the making of a special promise. The common elements here are those of acceptance and, more important, mutual commitment. Since the days of the ancient Greeks and Hebrews, the handclasp has expressed a covenant by which two parties pledge something (friendship, loyalty, commercial trust) to one another.

It is likely, though unprovable, that the earliest pledges were of nonaggression. Most handshaking is right-handed, and the joining of dominant hands could have demonstrated that neither party was about to use a weapon. The American Indian custom of greeting with the empty palm held high and the modern custom of waving may be survivals of the same primitive peace sign.

This interpretation would also explain why, until quite recently, it was chiefly males who practiced handshaking. Offering one's hand to a woman would carry the outrageous implication that the "gentler sex" too could be dangerous. It is now acceptable for American women to shake hands and even to do so firmly. But energetic handshaking is still largely a masculine activity. A strong grip signifies male bonding through a silent display of competitive power; the vertical shaking pattern, which may have arisen as a way of dislodging hidden weapons, also formalizes, and thus defuses, aggressive impulses.

The ritualized defusing of aggression is even more blatant in the Soviet Union than in the United States. According to Barbara Monahan, Russian men "often carry handshaking to an extreme," imparting "painful results but not permanent injury" to their comrades. Perhaps handshaking contests should be brought to Geneva as a way of furthering détente.

THE OK SIGN

When the forefinger and the thumb are joined in a circle, the American meaning is approval, a gesture signaling that something is "All right" or "Perfect." The sign has been linked to the expression "OK," as many call it the American OK sign, and take it as a representation of the letter "O." The problem with this interpretation is that only the expression "OK" is native to the United States. ("OK" dates from the 1840s and is probably an abbreviation of Martin Van Buren's nickname, Old Kinderhook, a reference to his birthplace in Kinderhook, New York.) The thumb and forefinger sign predates Van Buren's presidency by eighteen centuries: the first-century Roman rhetorician Quintilian, in his treatise on oratory, gives the gesture as a sign of approval.

It's clear, therefore, that the OK sign acquired its modern connotation in the ancient world and that the verbal expression was a late, and accidental, support. What remains to be explained is the symbolic logic involved. Morris and his colleagues draw a connection between the gesture and the thumb-to-forefinger "precision grip"; such a grip often emphasizes fine points in human conversation. The thumb and forefinger gesture is also among the commonest of *mudras*, or sacred finger postures, in the Buddhist and Hindu contemplative traditions; as such, it appropriately symbolizes the inner perfection that the meditator seeks to achieve. Finally, of course, there is the circle itself, one of the oldest and most common symbols for perfection in both Eastern and Western cultures. The unspoken message of the ancient sign may be simply, "That is as perfect as a circle."

CROSSING YOUR FINGERS

We cross our fingers in several different situations: when we are wishing for good luck (or wishing to avoid bad luck) and when we are saying something untrue for which we want to avoid being held accountable. The statements that go along with these situations are "Keep your fingers crossed" and "It doesn't count, I had my fingers crossed." These situations have in common the feature of potential danger; thus the gesture serves as protection from bad luck or from the penalties normally associated with lying.

Why should crossed fingers provide protection? Because they are what Desmond Morris and his colleagues call a "cryptic version" of the sign of the cross—a version early Christians could have employed without attracting the attention of pagan eyes. Only after its origins were obscured by longstanding repetition did the twined fingers pattern "come out into the open as a light-hearted social gesture, performed by Christians and non-Christians alike."

GIVING THE FINGER

W. S. King, studying California student gestures in 1949, called the erect middle finger "the most widely known symbol" among his informants. Recognizing it as an often joking sign of contempt, he also allowed that its meaning was "obscene." The specific obscenity was, then as now, one of phallic aggressiveness. Even if the visual form does not make this clear, the accompanying comments do. Typically the finger-flipper says, "Fuck you," or, if the intended insult is anal, "Up yours." Thus connotatively the gesture may be likened to the British palm-backward "V" sign and the generically European forearm jerk. The middle finger may have been chosen as a phallic symbol because as the longest digit, it is the most likely to be employed in genital and anal stimulation.

As popular as the gesture is in the United States, it is not an American invention. The Romans used it two thousand years ago, calling it *digitus impudicus,* "finger without shame." Modern Italians have carried on the Roman tradition as well, and so, in a peculiar variant, have the Russians. In the Soviet Union, bending back the middle finger of one hand with the forefinger of the other hand is close to but much coarser than the American sign. The gesture is called "looking under the cat's tail," and so the meaning is doubly offensive, suggesting not only sexual victimization but also inspection of a feline anus. It's a kind of obscene overkill.

THUMBS UP/THUMBS DOWN

When not being used in hitchhiking, the raised thumb gesture in our culture typically indicates approval. Popular wisdom links the gesture to the Roman arena, where the emperor and/or the mob supposedly spared a wounded gladiator's life by turning thumbs up and ordered death by turning thumbs down. This is "fakelore," deriving from the imprecise translation of the Latin term *pollice verso* ("with a turned thumb") as "with the thumb turned down." According to the second-century writer Juvenal, it was indeed with *pollice verso* that arena spectators condemned the unlucky, but there is no way of knowing whether *verso* meant turned up, turned down, or turned away. The preference of translators for "down" dates back only a century.

That preference was widely popularized—indeed, set in the public imagination—by the French classical genre painter Léon Gérôme, whose 1873 painting *Pollice Verso* showed an emperor making a "thumbs down" gesture. But there's a biological component involved too that's linked to the obvious but conceptually momentous fact that we are vertically oriented, bipedal animals. Sociobiologist Donald G. MacRae suggests some of the implications of this fact. Our conceptions of space and direction, he points out, "derive from our conception of the body and would not hold for an intelligent bilateral but horizontal animal, far less for a radially symmetrical one like a clever starfish." One basis of that conception is our up-and-down orientation. "Being upright," says MacRae, "seems a general convention of thought about being human." Implicit in that convention are the values attached to vertical position. "Up" (not to mention "upright") is better than "down," "high" is better than "low," "superior" is better than "inferior." Hence "thumbs up" is better than "thumbs down."

THE "V" SIGN

The palm-forward "V" sign, formed by raising and spreading the first two fingers, has had three distinct connotations in American culture. The oldest and least common is obscene. As a variant of the European "cuckold" or "horns" gesture, the "V" sign is a double phallic insult, meaning "Your wife has been cheating on you" or, when placed surreptitiously behind another's head, "His wife has been cheating on him." American children who jokingly "put horns" behind friends' heads in group snapshots are unknowingly reproducing something that southern Europeans would find highly offensive. (Russian children practice the same mischief, giving what they call "horns of the Devil.")

The second meaning of the "V" sign was invented in 1941 by Belgian propagandist Victor De Lavalaye. Wanting a symbol for resistance to the Nazi occupation, he came up with the single letter "V," which stood not only for his own first name, but also for English *victory,* Flemish *vrijheid,* and French *victoire.* The symbolism caught on rapidly and was immortalized by Winston Churchill, who used it constantly in public appearances. Thus throughout the 1940s and 1950s, the gesture meant simply "victory."

The most recent transformation came in the 1960s, when American antiwar protesters, sensitive to the military implication, used the sign sarcastically *against* the army, so that it became known as the "peace sign." In the 1970s, when the Vietnam War and hippiedom both wound down, the demilitarized "V" was a common greeting among Free Love faddists, acid heads, political radicals, and, ultimately, young people in general. By about the middle of the 1970s, it had become assimilated into the mainstream, so that it ceased to give clues to the user's philosophy.

In the United States, the gesture is typically given with the palm facing the viewer. The British use both this version and an older, palm-back version; the latter is obscene and corresponds to the American "finger" (see GIVING THE FINGER). Churchill got some unexpected stares in 1941 when, evidently unaware of the vulgar usage, he gave the palm-back "V" to British troops, saying, in effect, "Fuck you." In England today you would have to be a social hermit not to understand the distinction. Or maybe just a member of the insular ruling class: Astonishingly, Margaret

Thatcher repeated Churchill's error after her victory in the 1979 elections.

THUMBING YOUR NOSE

The nose-thumbing gesture—raising the thumb to the nose and extending the fingers in a fan—has two distinctions. It is the most widespread European finger gesture, and it is one of only a few gestures that are universally understood in the same way: Throughout America and Europe, thumbing the nose is virtually always a sign of mockery.

Desmond Morris and his colleagues suggest the following explanations of this common gesture. It is (1) a deformed salute, made by dropping the thumb from the horizontal position to the nose, (2) a modified stylization of thumbsucking, indicating that the recipient is a baby, (3) a mimicked threat of snot-flicking, (4) an indication of a grotesque or phallic nose, (5) the representation of a coxscomb— from which we get the common English expression "cocking a snoot" (snout), and (6) a stylized implication that someone stinks. Although I agree that it is unwise to favor one particular source for this gesture, I incline toward the first and last explanations.

CROSSING YOUR HEART

There is an old folk tradition in which a person making a promise would "seal" it by crossing his heart—that is, by drawing an "X" over his breast. This tradition was a secularization of an even older gestural tradition: the religious tradition of crossing oneself that still exists in the Roman and Orthodox Catholic churches. Crossing the heart, like crossing the fingers, provides protection against bad luck by invoking the power of the holy object. At the same time, it invokes the savior on the cross as a witness that the speaker's pledge is in earnest. Breaking such a pledge would put the speaker's soul in jeopardy; hence the solemn caution: "Cross my heart and hope to die" (if my pledge proves false).

It its religious form (actually, forms), crossing has been around almost since the beginning of Christianity. A thumb and index finger forehead cross was customary in the second century as a private devotion. The devotion had become liturgical by the fourth century, and the breast (that is, the heart) was also crossed. Full-body crossing came in around the fifth century and was adopted widely by monks in the tenth. Following prescriptions laid down by Pope Innocent III in the thirteenth century, Eastern-rite Catholics today cross themselves with the thumb and first two fingers (symbolizing the trinity) and they touch the right shoulder first. Roman-rite followers touch the left shoulders first and use all five digits—representing, perhaps, Christ's five wounds.

PRAYING HANDS

When addressing a deity, most people stretch their arms out wide to the sky, inviting the divine presence in as if through a kind of funnel. This exhibitionist form of divine address has never been very popular in America. Following the individualized, Protestant tenor of religion here, Christians use the more discreet hand press, either in the traditional first communion gesture, with the palms touching and the fingers pointing upward, or with the hands clasped in a loose double fist.

There are several possible meanings for this gesture. First, as a variant of what Ray Birdwhistell calls the "steepling" gesture, the finger press may symbolize contemplation, just as the more open fingertip-style steepling does. Second, as a variant of the traditional Hindu greeting posture—in which the greeter bows over praying hands to his acquaintance, the gesture may be a Western reflection of an Indo-European communion pose. Third, the gesture may be a subtle pointing motion: In the most stylized form of the finger posture, all ten digits point upward, as if "shooting" the supplicant's message in the right direction. Fourth, the handclasp or finger press might be seen as one segment of a more dynamic megagesture—the systole of a hand-motion pattern whose diastole is the outstretching of arms. Popes use this in-out-in-out "breathing" pattern frequently, and the devout may be unconsciously mimicking their motions. Finally, the gesture may be seen as a stylized modification of the most self-absorbed type of prayer posture, where the supplicant holds his face in his hands. Like the outstretched-hands posture, this extremely private posture, which looks like a "Woe is me" signal to fellow prayers, might be simply too ostentatious in a culture that prides itself on "inner light."

SCRATCHING YOUR HEAD

Few instances of head scratching are caused by dandruff or lice. In most cases, we scratch our heads, or sometimes the back of our necks, because we are skeptical or confused. Desmond Morris (1985) relates the gesture to "frustrated aggression," suggesting that it is derived from our "primeval attack movement." In modern hand-to-hand combat, the sophisticated, learned frontal punch is more commonly employed than the overarm blow. But in instances of "natural" anger, such as nursery tantrums and street rioting, we use the apelike high-arc movement. It is this movement that is being displayed, and then immediately disguised, when we raise a hand to the top or the back of the head.

SHRUGGING YOUR SHOULDERS

Charles Darwin explained the shoulder shrug by the "principle of unconscious antithesis." An indignant person, ready to fight for home or honor, holds his head upright, squares his shoulders, and clenches his fists. A person who feels incapable or uncertain adopts an opposite posture. He hunches his shoulders, tilts his head, and shows his hands palm upward. The message is one of helplessness: "I don't know what to say" or "I couldn't help it." The shoulder shrug has also been defined as a form of defensive hunching or symbolic retreat from an unmanageable situation. Raising the shoulders has the apparent effect of lowering the head. The careless, half-humorous shrug thus bears a visual affinity to the nod or bow of submissiveness and also to a turtle's retraction of its head into its shell. Whether or not our neurological wiring is mimicking our reptilian past here, the meaning of the shrug among humans is the same as that among turtles: "This is too much for me to handle."

GENUFLECTION

In Islam the ultimate abasement before the Almighty is full-body prostration. In the West this extreme is rare; we settle for the single- or double-leg kneel. As a body-lowering device, the kneel serves the same symbolic purpose as the bow: It demonstrates subservience to a superior, such as a sovereign, a lord, or God. The single-leg kneel has long been the prescribed form for abasement before mere humans, and the full, or double-leg, kneel has been reserved for the deity. One gives a brief, single-leg kneel to a Catholic altar—a genuflection or knee bend—only when one is walking by; a longer stay (in a pew, for example) requires the full double kneel.

It is worthwhile noting one variant of the basically religious genuflection. Raymond Firth observes that the curtsy, or courtesy, arose in the sixteenth century, and that by the nineteenth century it had become the standard submissive posture for young women. A kind of semigenuflection, it displays instability as well as submission; thus it subtly endorses the "weaker sex" stereotype.

WINKING

As a sign of momentary collusion between intimates, winking is common throughout Europe and America. The implication of the gesture is that the winker and the winkee share a secret or at least a private understanding of a public situation. Desmond Morris (1985) considers the action "directional eye closure." He explains, "Closing the eye suggests that the secret is aimed only at the person being looked at. The other eye is kept open for the rest of the world, who are excluded from the private exchange." An opposite interpretation might also work: The winker keeps one eye on the winkee, while symbolically shutting everyone else out.

STICKING OUT YOUR TONGUE

People stick out their tongues as a way of dealing with social interactions that are unpleasant for them. These interactions may range from the potential disruption of an activity requiring close concentration—hence the tongue-showing of children who are entirely focused on their schoolwork—to the unwelcome advance of a suitor, in which case the tongue display is overtly insulting. There are two common, and not necessarily mutually exclusive, explanations of why this display indicates rejection.

The simple, developmental explanation is that tongue-showing reflects the infantile mouth movement of nipple rejection, displayed when a baby is tired of suckling. Connecting the gesture to early feeding in this way has the extra benefit of explaining why the tongue is used to invite, as well as repulse, sexual contact: When we stick out our tongues to lick our lips, we are replicating the movement of the infant's exploring tongue, mimicking its search for the breast, and saying, in effect, "You look good enough to eat."

A more symbolic explanation is that in pointing a tongue out in insult, we are displaying a substitute phallus. Erection display among apes is a typical component of aggression, and throughout many traditional cultures, as Irenäus Eibl-Eibesfeldt shows, figures displaying prominent erections are used as intimidating "scarecocks." Since American law frowns on phallic exhibitionism, we learn to exhibit insult and rejection more indirectly, with the tongue.

RAISING YOUR EYEBROWS

Alertness in horses and dogs is demonstrated by the raising of ears and the flaring of nostrils. Human beings, like other primates, rely more on sight than on either smell or hearing, and so when we are alerted, it is our eyes that go up. Not only do our pupils dilate, but the eyebrows themselves arch upward, as a register of recognition or surprise. Many biologists consider eyebrow-raising to be a ritualized attention-getting device. This is relevant whether the social interaction involved is greeting, surprise, approval, flirting, gratitude, or simple emphasis. Even when the gesture is used haughtily, by a supercilious (literally, "above the eyebrow") person, the element of increased attention remains: the translation of the arching gesture of the "highbrow" is "I am trying to take this all in, but I cannot believe you are so stupid."

Desmond Morris (1985) calls the eyebrow raise a "vision improving device." But he acknowledges a puzzle, because both eyebrow lowering and raising typically are associated with increased attention and specifically with attention to a possible threat. Raising the brows improves vision, and lowering them protects the eyes, so ironically these opposite gestures both serve as techniques of defense. The problem, according to Morris, is that when faced with a threat, "the brain has to assess which is the more important demand and instruct the face accordingly." Morris's ingenious explanation of the neural logic involved here derives from observation of primates. When a baboon or a human is extremely aggressive or extremely submissive—that is, when he fears that a physical confrontation is imminent—he lowers his brows to protect his eyes. When he is only slightly aggressive and also scared—that is, when he has not yet decided whether to fight or to run—"he sacrifices eye protection for the tactical advantages of being able to see more clearly," and his eyebrows go up.

NODDING YES, SHAKING NO

Although not universal, a vertical head nod for approval and a lateral headshake for negation is a common pattern across many cultures. Most biologists agree with Charles Darwin that the two movements mimic infantile nursing patterns. The forward head nod is seen as part of the breast-seeking or breast-accepting pattern, and the headshaking gesture as the infant's pattern of refusal. The negation pattern, of course, lasts into the toddler years, when the child says no to an offered spoon.

A sociobiological explanation, offered by Irenäus Eibl-Eibesfeldt, suggests that the affirmative vertical nod may be connected to "ritualized submission," in which we "submit to the ideas of the speaker," and that the negative lateral shake may derive from the shaking-off movement of birds and mammals. We refuse an uncongenial idea in the same manner that a wet dog rejects the water. These ingenious, if unprovable, suggestions do not in any case discredit the nursing hypothesis.

That the yes-no gesture contrast is probably infantile and not culturally implanted later on is supported by the fact that children who are born deaf and blind fall naturally into the pattern without modeling.

RITES OF PASSAGE:

TRANSITIONS

PASSING OUT CIGARS

The father's distribution of cigars after the arrival of a baby may be seen as a small, modern variant of primitive reallocation ceremonies like the Northwest Coast Indian *potlatch,* in which an individual blessed with good fortune shares it with the community as a way of avoiding the envy of both his fellows and the gods. Indirectly it may also have something to do with sacrifice. Just as the ancient Mayans blew tobacco smoke toward the sun to appease their gods, the smoke of the proud papa's cigars may be expected to waft toward the heavens, in fragrant and communal thanksgiving. In this sense the cigar smoke serves the same purpose as any other burnt offering—to delight the nostrils of the powers that be. Of course, the most obvious interpretation of the cigar-giving ritual is the Freudian one. It is a brag. By handing out all those phallic images, the father is acknowledging his own part in the birth and advertising his generative potency.

BAPTISM

The word *baptism* comes from the Greek *baptein,* meaning "to dip," and it refers to the ceremony of admitting a person into Christianity by immersing him in water to symbolically wash away sin. In Biblical history, the model for this custom is the dipping of Jesus in the Jordan by his herald, St. John the Baptist. Whether of the full-immersion (dipping) or font (sprinkling) variety, Christians of all denominations practice water baptism because of this historical model and because of Jesus's comment in John 3:5 that "unless a man be born again of water and the Holy Spirit, he cannot enter into the Kingdom of God."

The Christian church today carefully distinguishes its form of baptism from the many non-Christian varieties that preceded it. Thus, from the *New Catholic Encyclopedia* baptism is "the sacramental representation of the death and resurrection of Jesus Christ"; it is not to be confused with the "ritual bath of late Judaism" or with the initiatory cleansing rites of the pagan religions. Yet surely the encyclopedia doth protest too much. As J. A. MacCulloch showed in his survey of ethnic baptism among traditional peoples, water baptism has been extremely common throughout the world from very ancient times and has always functioned dually, as purification and protection. Purification was necessary after a birth because birthing women were considered unclean or taboo because of "the mystery which surrounds certain periodic or occasional functions of woman's life," that is, menstruation and child delivery. Although some cultures purified their women by seclusion or fumigation, the most common method was ritual washing. Protection was necessary at the same time, because the newborn and its mother were considered in danger from evil spirits. Again, the water of life was the natural agent to combat their baneful powers.

It is a small conceptual jump from these traditional ideas about preventing contagion and thwarting evil to the more "sophisticated" Christian notion that baptismal water washes away original sin. Indeed, given the common confusion among Christians between carnality and culpability, baptism might well be seen as the corrective to the "evil" of reproduction. It is appropriate that baptismal water is likened to the "blood of the Lamb," since that pure, sacrificial blood is the perfect agent to replace the "fallen" blood of menses and mortal birth.

In Christian baptism, as in its pagan forerunners, the ceremony often includes naming—or renaming, in the case of adult ceremonies. Since baptism is a typical passage rite, this also makes sense. The child who is born into this fallen world in effect "dies" during the baptismal rite, and is reborn into Christ at its ending. The evidence of that rebirth is its (new) name.

GODPARENTS

Today the office of godparent is frequently a secular one, since many couples who are not religious and who do not even have their children baptised still see fit to designate a relative or a trusted friend as potential guardian of their infant's welfare should something happen to them. The charge to many godparents today is simply, "Take good care of my child." Yet the custom of choosing godparents, as the term indicates, is inherently religious, and in the Catholic faith, where the custom originated, it is still a very serious matter. The official Church term for godparents is *sponsors,* and the charge of the sponsors is quite precise: they are to oversee the child's religious upbringing. This obligation exists even when the parents are alive; so it's obvious that the duty of godparents, as originally construed, is to be spiritual advisers who will not be swayed by parental softness into bending the spirit of the law.

CIRCUMCISION

The word *circumcision* comes from the Latin for "cutting around." In everyday usage it means the surgical removal of the foreskin, or prepuce, of a male infant's penis. This curious operation, which is standard procedure in most American hospitals, is usually defended on the grounds of hygiene, because of the belief that an uncircumcised penis is prone to infection, but, as Rosemary Romberg points out in her 1985 manifesto against the practice, intact males do not suffer a significantly higher risk of infection (or of penile cancer) when they routinely wash under the foreskin. Infection results from incomplete personal hygiene, not any supposed dirtiness of the uncircumcised organ itself. The American bias toward cutting rather than washing merely reflects the medical establishment's bias toward surgery and its traditional disdain for patient education.

Before about 1900, Rosemary Romberg points out, most non-Jewish American and European males were uncircumcised. Circumcision was adopted gradually as a result of the Victorian obsession with masturbation and the medical community's belief that this "pollution" could be restrained by the removal of foreskins. British surgeon James Hutchinson was the point man in the spread of the practice. His 1891 paper "On Circumcision as Preventative of Masturbation" is generally accepted as the first position paper for routine modern infant circumcision.

But, of course, circumcision is not a modern practice; nor have male infants been its only recipients. Mutilation of both male and female genitals is a widespread custom in tribal societies, and because it often takes place during adolescence rather than infancy, the common anthropological view is that it is a ritual of puberty and fertility. Romberg suggests that in addition to this standard interpretation, in ancient times circumcision may have functioned as symbolic castration, as a means of diminishing (or enhancing) sexual desire, as status identification, as a sign of bravery, as a mirror of menstruation (reflecting "womb envy"), and as a mark of tribal identity.

BIRTHDAY SPANKINGS

When our children administer mock spankings to a birthday boy or girl, they are recalling the beating and flagellation rites of preindustrial cultures—rites that anthropologists have long identified as integral features of many initiation ceremonies. In his classic study *Rites of Passage,* French ethnographer Arnold Van Gennep pointed out that all initiation rites follow a predictable three-phase pattern of separation from the community, indoctrination, and reentry. The attacks on the initiate's body that often highlight this triadic pattern both purify the initiate and identify the gravity of the transition.

Today the separation-and-reincorporation pattern is most evident in wedding and honeymoon rituals, but even the ordinary birthday party, since it is clearly a rite of passage, also provides glimpses of the structure. The communal public spanking puts a twist on the ancient wisdom by, in effect, isolating the birthday child psychologically, subjecting him to a humiliating hazing ritual that highlights his specialness, and then inviting him back to the fold by offering luck, one to grow on, and congratulations.

"HAPPY BIRTHDAY TO YOU"

Traditionally sung just before the birthday boy or girl blows out the candles on the cake, this refrain is so simple, in melody and lyric, that children of three can sing it without hesitation. This is appropriate, because the composers of the song were long involved in elementary education. They were Mildred and Patty Smith Hill, the daughters of a progressive Kentucky couple who believed in female education at a time—the mid-nineteenth century—when it was still a novel idea and who trained their two girls to be schoolteachers. Mildred's career was obscure, but Patty achieved considerable prominence as a pioneer in kindergarten education and was for several decades a major spokesperson for preschool education. She taught at Columbia University's Teachers College from 1905 to 1935, and at her retirement became one of the first women to be named a professor emeritus by Columbia.

The song, with its original title "Good Morning to You," was written by the two sisters in 1893. Its appropriation, without permission, into a 1921 Irving Berlin/Moss Hart Broadway play led to a successful lawsuit against the producers.

BIRTHDAY CANDLES

In her survey of birthday lore, Linda Rannells Lewis suggests that the birthday candle may derive, distantly, from the ancient Greek practice of offering to Artemis, goddess of the hunt and of the moon, a round honey cake into which a candle had been stuck. After German bakers invented the modern birthday cake in the Middle Ages, a similar custom was adopted for the invocation of good spirits at birthdays. The cake, ready by morning, would be surrounded by burning candles, in a kind of protective fire circle, and they would be kept lit all day, until dessert time at the evening meal. A variant of this custom was the use of a huge, twelve-year taper, one-twelfth to be consumed on each birthday, until the child became an "adult" at thirteen.

All these customs contain elements of reverence and, probably, of propitiation. Candles typically are used at solemn events, such as funerals and church services, but Lewis observes that even at joyous birthdays the suggestion of death is present. Each birthday, after all, is another step toward the end, and what we celebrate at birthday gatherings is not only our growth but our transience. Thus, in Lewis's words, "Candles are symbols of dualities, life and death, light in the darkness, fragile hopes and overpowering fears, the warmth of a protected hearth and the horror of an uncontrolled inferno, increase and loss, sex and sacrifice, a prayer to the gods and God's all-seeing eye."

In view of this, the candle-blowing-out ritual dramatizes a central human query: To what extent do we control our own lives? By making a wish over the symbols of our progress, we invoke powers beyond ourselves for continued benefits. When we actively snuff out those symbols, we demonstrate our complicity in—and our hope for a degree of control over—whatever the gods may have in store.

FIRST HOLY COMMUNION

Roman Catholic children, often dressed in traditional white for joy and purity, receive their First Holy Communion around their seventh or eighth birthday. This custom is now well established, but it is interesting to note that, viewed against the broad backdrop of Church history, it is an invention of the Middle Ages. Before the thirteenth century, children were admitted to Communion at baptism, which meant that they only had a sip of wine, since they were too young to negotiate the bread. However, they were barred from this traditional participation in 1215, when the fourth Lateran Council ruled that before partaking of the Body of Christ, a communicant had to know what it was: Children could be given Communion only after they understood the distinction between plain bread and the Bread of Life. That sounds sensible enough until you recall that it was precisely the inability of adults to agree on this distinction that created countless heresies and ultimately the Protestant Reformation. Perhaps because they understand the dilemma involved here, Church leaders now take seven or eight as an a priori "age of discretion" or "age of reason," without requiring each little communicant to solve the problem that perplexed Martin Luther.

BAR MITZVAH

The Hebrew term *bar mitzvah* translates as "son of the command-ment," although in popular usage the expression refers to the cere-mony *making* one a son of the commandment. In this ceremony, which occurs by tradition on the day after the Jewish boy's thir-teenth birthday, he becomes a full member of the religious commu-nity and is fully subject to Jewish law. Specifically, this means that he may be a member of a *minyan* (the quorum of ten males needed for a traditional congregational service), that he may buy and sell property, and that he must wear the *tefillin* (leather prayer boxes) on his person while praying.

Although the bar mitzvah tradition was not officially established until the fifteenth century—and the equivalent *bat mitzvah* ("daugh-ter of the commandment") ceremony not until the nineteenth cen-tury—the importance of the age of thirteen as a turning point has been implicit in Jewish life since Biblical times. Abraham rejected the idols of his father at this age, and it was at thirteen that Jacob and Esau parted ways. Jewish law fixed thirteen as the age of responsi-bility because it was considered the time of physical and mental maturity for boys. Thus the bar mitzvah rite, unlike the Holy Com-munion rite of the Catholic Church, is a puberty ceremony as well as a religious incorporation. Often this aspect is referred to obliquely in the public address that the "bar mitzvah" is required by custom to give to the congregation. In traditional Jewish families the boy delivers an official *derashah,* or "Talmudic discourse." In less tradi-tional settings, the speech may emphasize the young man's religious and secular coming of age. The standard opening line for such a speech is still "Today I am a man."

SWEET SIXTEEN PARTIES

In an era when teenage pregnancy is only slightly less common than acne, the quaint expression "sweet sixteen and never been kissed" has a somewhat cynical ring. It arose at a time when teenage sex was not nearly as common as it is today, and when a girl might easily reach her sixteenth birthday without having gotten much beyond the flirting stage. The sweet sixteen parties of that more innocent time served as a kind of puberty initiation rite. At the ones I attended in the 1950s, it was generally assumed that if the birthday girl had not been kissed yet, the deficiency would be corrected before the party ended. The popular association in those days between the magic age of sixteen and awakening desire was reflected in a raft of popular songs, from Sam Cooke's "Only Sixteen" to the Crests' "Sixteen Candles" to Chuck Berry's rollicking teen anthem, "Sweet Little Sixteen."

Why sixteen should have been chosen as a borderline is open to speculation. Possibly it is because the number five is a common delimiting figure (Five Year Plans, five workdays), and sixteen begins the fourth "set of five" in the young person's chronology. It may also be considered important as the midpoint of the teen years, or as a symbolic age of puberty: The onset of menses occurs usually at eleven or twelve today, but it was about sixteen a century ago.

COMING-OUT PARTIES

Etiquette maven Judith Martin (1982) ridicules the modern coming-out party, or "deb dance," as a committee-mismanaged extravaganza in which "fond parents are able to attach a permanent date to their daughter's youth, have her scrutinized by strangers, and arrange for her to meet a lot of young men who have come to believe that the world owes them free champagne." It was, she says, not always so. In the mid-nineteenth century, when the idea of the coming-out party came to fruition, the intention was to introduce one's daughter to one's own circle of friends—not the social leaders of some nearby moneyopolis—and, quite incidentally, to show her off to those friends' eligible sons. Today the mating dance aspect of the tradition has overwhelmed the more social features, and even worse, the garish tastes of the adolescents themselves often are permitted to override parental designs.

The idea of debutante parties may have a very ancient origin. Lillian Eichler (1924) argues convincingly that the first debutantes were primitive maidens who had reached puberty but who still had to endure a period of seclusion before being permitted to marry. Citing evidence from Africa and the South Seas, she suggests that many women actually were kept in cages before marriage, and that the feasting that occurred upon their release was a prototype of the modern deb dance.

HAZING

Whether it's part of a high school or college freshman "Hell Week" or part of a fraternity pledging rite, the submitting of the young to indignities at the hands of the not-quite-so-young—or "hazing"—is part of a long university tradition that is part of the broader tradition of rites of passage. In certain African societies, when a boy comes of age, he is handed a spear, pointed in the direction of the bush, and told to come back with a dead lion. Only after passing this test of endurance and bravery is he designated an adult. The hazing rituals of adolescent students constitute a modern, somewhat sanitized version of such primitive tests. Their fundamental logic is that the "new kids" must prove themselves worthy of moving to the next level, that is, college or fraternity status. The difference between the modern and the primitive rituals is that lion-killing serves a practical function in societies that require it while hazing serves only a psychological function: it creates and reinforces the illusion that performing ridiculous and self-debasing acts magically undoes one's adolescence. The irony of hazing is that freshmen or fraternity pledges are proving their manhood by behaving in an infantile fashion.

A more logical explanation of this process is that hazing does not reinforce initiative, or the ability to be a "good sport," but precisely that subservience to authority that any good conformist culture depends on. Henry D. Sheldon, observing late-nineteenth-century hazing at Amherst College, understood it as a demonstration of "the conservatism and reverence for tradition which marks the earliest period of youth." In other words, the college pledge wears a dress on Main Street for the same reason that the African boy hunts the lion: He believes that he has no choice.

FRATERNITY PINNING

Sporting a beau's fraternity pin, like wearing a beau's high school ring around one's neck, is a sign that a young woman is "almost"

betrothed or "engaged to be engaged." As fraternity historian Clyde
Johnson points out, the founders of the American fraternity system
would have been surprised and confused to find the emblems of their
creation used in this way. The eighteenth- and nineteenth-century
fraternity houses were bastions of exclusive male privilege, and the
system itself had been developed for political and social reasons.
Throughout the nineteenth century, as the Greek system took hold
on various campuses, fraternity members retained a good deal of the
founders' religious and reformist zeal. The idea behind the system,
Johnson writes, was "to enhance individual liberties, to broaden the
opportunities for student participation, and to correct . . . abuses,
unfairness, and hypocrisy in campus affairs." The rowdiness, sexism,
and racism that today's Animal Houses are associated with developed gradually throughout the nineteenth century and were certainly not part of the original design.

The fraternity pin, which initially betokened membership in a
secret, ennobling brotherhood, came to be used for romantic purposes after women became part of the college system, in the first
couple of decades after the Civil War. Gradually the intellectual and
moral aspirations of the fraternity system were eased out by the more
immediate concerns of commerce, pleasure, and romance, and the
chapter house, no longer an arena for avant-garde ideas, became a
place to meet future business partners and wives. Social standing
played a major part in this mercantilization of the Greek system, and
the pinning ritual came to be not only a codification of puppy love,
but an element of ceremonial bonding among eligible young people
of the "right" class. With the rise of sororities late in the century,
the opportunities for making appropriate matches through the Greek
system were dramatically increased, and the exchange of pins became a secular first step in "proper" courtship. At the same time,
according to John Findley Scott, the indirect but strict control of
sororities by status-conscious alumnae helped to protect easily in-
fatuated young women from "the stratum-dissolving standards of
the larger university," encouraging them to "marry up."

Thus, informally and indirectly, the Greek system serves as
marriage broker, and the fraternity pin serves as an announcement of eligibility and social ranking. In giving this status symbol to
another, you are saying, "You are worthy of being a member of my
clan."

CAPS AND GOWNS

The caps and gowns worn by high school and college graduates today are survivors of the everyday dress worn by members of the academic community in medieval Europe. The majority of scholars in the Middle Ages were churchmen, or soon to become so, and their dress was often strictly regulated by the universities where they taught and studied. Ordinary dress throughout Europe was the long *cappa* or cope that was standard clerical garb. According to a directive of 1215 cited by Lynn Thorndike, "None of the masters lecturing in arts shall have a cope except one round, black and reaching to the ankles." Nor could scholars wear "shoes that are ornamented or with elongated pointed toes." The original preference of ecclesiastical authorities for black, Hastings Rashdall said, was modified in the thirteenth and fourteenth centuries, as red, violet, and purple hues came in; but by the Renaissance black was back in, "a symbol of the way in which sixteenth-century austerity eclipsed the warmth and colour of medieval life." With few exceptions, modern universities retain that ceremonial austerity.

The origin of the square flat cap, or mortarboard, is obscure, although it probably derives from the medieval biretta, a tufted square cap which, Rashdall said, was "the distinctive badge of the mastership" and was only later appropriated by undergraduates and schoolboys. The term *mortarboard* did not appear in English until the 1850s. The tassel that graduates transfer from one side to another as a signal of their elevation is an outgrowth of the medieval tuft. The tuft still appears on the modern biretta, worn by bishops throughout the Church of Rome.

THE RETIREMENT WATCH

Receiving an engraved timepiece as a reward for decades of service to a firm seems, at first glance, like an ironic and almost taunting good-bye gesture. Why give the honored retiree something that, no longer a slave to nine-to-five, he will have so little use for? The answer, I suspect, lies not in the watch's utility, but in its function as a middle-class status symbol. In the nineteenth-century, the corner grocer or the third-assistant factory manager might not have

been able to afford the jewels of the upper class, but he could appease
this lust for status with a pocket watch. With its engraved lid and
dangling chain, it could function as a utilitarian ornament demonstrating both that its owner could tell time and that he was working
his way toward a pinky ring. Conferring such an honor on a retiring
employee acknowledged his social, not just his labor, value. It may
thus have served as an opiate for overworked laborers who might
otherwise have questioned the system. Potential owners of pocket
watches were no more likely to rock the boat than potential owners
of Rolexes are today.

RETIRING TO FLORIDA

The Spanish explorer Ponce de Leon went to Florida looking for the
Fountain of Youth, and for the past three generations millions of
Americans have followed his lead. Florida has by far the oldest
average population in the country, and it's getting older all the time.
In the early 1980s, more than one fourth of the state's 9 million
residents were over sixty years of age, and a full 17 percent were past
the traditional retirement age of sixty-five (compared to 11 percent
of the national population). Senior clubs, "adults only" condomini-
ums, and silver-haired legislators abound in the state. The dominance of nonagenarian Claude Pepper in the United States Senate,
especially with regard to the rights of elders, is a direct result of
Florida's senior citizen population. According to Florida-watcher
Paul Zach, for thousands of new retirees each month, the state
represents "their just reward for decades of labor in the landlocked
and seasonally cold northern states."

All this is pretty well known. What is not so well known is that
the Florida retirement syndrome owes its genesis to electronic technology, that is, to the fans and air-conditioning units that eventually
made the climate tolerable to Yankees. That happened in the 1930s,
which not at all incidentally was when the "grandparent boom" got
started. It is an ironic footnote that among the earlier, pre-air-condi-
tioning Florida vacationers was New Jersey's electricity whiz,
Thomas Edison. He went there for his health. Today's retirees go
there for the same reason, and because of the state's favorable tax
laws.

BLACK FOR MOURNING

Leopold Wagner said that black expresses "the solemn midnight gloom, the total deprivation of light and joy on account of the loss sustained." That common enough assessment explains why in many areas of the world black has long been thought the appropriate shade for mourning. But this preference is by no means universal. The Chinese color is white (for hope), the Persian brown (for withered leaves), the Syrian blue (for heaven) and even in the West the association of black with mourning is relatively new. Throughout the Middle Ages in Europe, the dominant mourning color was white, reflecting, perhaps, a hopeful attitude toward death. The mourning color changed only in 1498, when King Charles VIII of France died from a blow on the head and his widow, Anne of Brittany, donned unconventional black in his honor. The royal example started a vogue that has continued in the West ever since.

FLOWERS FOR THE DEAD

Since flowers symbolize new life, it may seem inappropriate to have them at funerals. Yet people in many cultures top caskets with wreaths and garlands and put blossoms on the graves of the departed. This custom is part of a widespread, long-lived pattern. Edwin Daniel Wolff speculated that floral tributes to the dead are an outgrowth of the grave goods of ancient times. In cultures that firmly believed in an afterlife, and that believed further that the departed could enter that afterlife only if they took with them indications of their worldly status, it was a necessity to bury the dead with material goods: hence the wives and animals that were killed to accompany dead rulers, the riches buried with Egyptian pharaohs, and the coins that Europeans used to place on the departed person's eyes as payment for the Stygian ferryman. In time, as economy modified tradition, the actual grave goods were replaced by symbolic representations. In China, for example, gold and silver paper became a stand-in for real money. Eventually even the symbolic significance became obscured. Thus, Wolff said, flowers may be the final step in "three well-marked stages of offerings to the dead: the actual object, its substitute in various forms, and—finally—mere tributes of respect."

COFFINS AND CASKETS

Since the casket accounts for a major part of the expense of the modern funeral, it is not surprising that the spread in popularity of caskets coincided almost exactly with the rise of the undertaking industry in the middle of the nineteenth century. The adoption of metal caskets at that time was promoted partly as a means of discouraging grave robbers—those ex officio minions of the medical schools—and partly as a way of preserving the body against the ravages of the earth; but the bottom line under both these rationales was the financial one: metal caskets brought in more money than wooden coffins.

People had been buried in coffins before that, but not for as long as is generally supposed. The ancient Egyptians buried their dead in coffins, and some burial mounds from early medieval England contain hollowed-out logs used as coffins. But it wasn't until the seventeenth century that burial in coffins became a widespread custom in Europe. Until then, all but the very wealthy were buried merely in shrouds. Many exceptions to this rule were in evidence during the 1665 plague in England, and perhaps that was what started the new style.

Once the custom was started, it was nearly a century before it took hold in its present form in the United States. Until the middle of the eighteenth century, American coffins typically were constructed by the friends and family of the deceased or by local cabinetmakers who knew the family. The specialized coffin manufacturer was a product of the late eighteenth century, and the high-water mark of his art— the gleaming, silken-padded metal casket that is designed to suggest a comfortable bed—is a product of only this century.

THE WAKE

Henry Bourne, complaining in 1725 about the riotousness of wakes, suggested that the word itself came from the Saxon term *wak,* signifying "drunkenness." His etymology was peculiar, but his objection was not. "Wake" is actually a form of "watch," indicating the nocturnal vigil of mourners or what Bourne himself called "watching with the dead." Such vigils were common from ancient times (the

Greeks, Romans, and Hebrews all had them), and the drunken variety, conventionally identified with the Irish, had, by Bourne's day, been piquing the pious for centuries. The ninth-century abbot Regino complained about the practical jokes, dances, and "diabolical songs" that were already common at these drunken vigils. Puritan counsel notwithstanding, the riotousness lasted into this century: My Irish mother recalls wakes in the 1930s that turned into quite festive occasions.

On one level, such display is merely distasteful. On another, it serves a psychological function, albeit a sad and defensive one: to deny the reality of the obvious, to put on a clown's face to keep from crying. There may also be a social function, however, that relates to primitive beliefs about the dead. Robert Habenstein and William Lamers note the medieval custom of "rousing the ghost," which included frightening superstitious relatives and "taking liberties with the corpse." The hidden impulse here seems not so much to shock or ridicule as to test whether or not the corpse is really dead—and to do so in a way that can be laughed off when it fails. In the days before embalming had become widespread, premature burial was not unknown, and a chief reason for having a "watch" at all, instead of burying the body immediately, was to guard against this horrifying possibility. Having a high old time at the funeral, therefore, served not only to give the deceased a good sendoff, but also to rouse him from slumber if there was still a chance of that happening.

FUNERAL PARLOR VIEWING

Bodies have been laid out since ancient times, and in this country until very recently they were set out for viewing not in a funeral parlor, but in the parlor of one's home. Until well into the nineteenth century the washing, dressing, and laying out of the body were commonly performed by the deceased person's own family. Even after the preparation of the body became professionalized after the Civil War, the viewing and the wake usually still took place in the household "parlor."

It would take a sociologist to explain why this no longer happens, and the best I can do in this context is to point to historical possibilities. Richard Huntington and Peter Metcalf say that with the advent of embalming and its accompanying technical apparatus, it became impractical to carry out the procedure in the deceased's home, and from there the undertaker must have considered it a natural next step to provide premises for the "viewing." But there is no reason that a body can't be embalmed in a funeral home and then taken to the deceased's home; that's exactly what happened in the 1950s funerals I remember.

The explanation given by Leroy Bowman may get closer to the truth. He relates the passing of the home viewing to increased urbanism and mobility, including social mobility. It is harder to hold a proper wake in a small city apartment than it is to hold it in a farmhouse. City dwellers, who comprise a larger and larger proportion of the population, hence often opt for the professional parlor. In addition, as business dealings get more spread out, as a person's circle of friends and acquaintances widens, and as relatives get geographically more scattered, the home ceases to be the focus of social life. Those events that once naturally took place there may be handed over to a funeral director who has the expertise needed for handling such a large and varied group of mourners.

EMBALMING

Ancient embalming meant the preservation of the body with aromatic oils, the chief of which was balsam or "balm." The modern method, which involves the replacement of body fluids by chemicals, was first patented in this country in 1856 by a Washington, D.C., entrepreneur named J. Anthony Gaussardia. Ten rival patents soon followed, most of them issued to other Washingtonians, and the nation's capital soon became the center of the American embalming industry.

This happened at an opportune moment, for Union soldiers were expiring by the hundreds far from home, and the new process provided a method of preserving their remains during the slow railroad and wagon trips home. The federal government's original policy had been to bury its dead on the battlefield; civilian protests made that policy politically unwise, and embalming made it unnecessary. Preserving the war dead boosted the fortunes of the then nascent funeral industry, since it gave novice undertakers so many bodies to use their newly learned skills on.

What really turned America on to the funeral industry was the embalming of the assassinated President Lincoln. Lincoln's preserved corpse was viewed by thousands of Americans on its way home from Washington to Springfield, Illinois, and this national viewing started a vogue.

THE CORPSE'S LIFELIKE APPEARANCE

One of the dubious advantages afforded bereaved Americans by the nineteenth-century science of embalming was the ability to transform a shrunken, ashen face into the picture of premorbid health. The restorative techniques, both surgical and chemical, that morticians began to employ about a century ago led gradually to the modern custom of displaying an uncannily "lifelike" corpse. This permits mourners looking into the casket to comment on how much "like himself" poor old Uncle Harry looks. What they mean is that unwrinkled and unblemished, Harry looks five or ten years younger than he did when he died.

It is no accident that gazing on his "fully restored" countenance, some grievers are moved to announce that he looks "almost alive." On a fundamental ceremonial level, this is the point of the restoration: to suggest that science has reversed the inevitable.

Leroy Bowman says the funeral industry's rationale for this custom is that the powdered visage helps the survivors; as an eleventh-hour but durable "memory image," it is "of great and lasting value in bereavement and the adjustment process." Unfortunately, there is no psychological evidence that viewing a youthful-looking corpse has any greater bereavement value than does viewing an unrejuvenated one, and this lack of evidence has led many observers to see facial restoration as just one more ploy by the undertaker to hike up the funeral bill. Another interpretation sees restoration as part of the wholesale denial of death that infuses our culture at large: we ask our corpses to look younger for the same reason that we pad coffins and refuse, with few exceptions, to allow deaths at home: we must deny the brute facts of mortality and putrefaction. Finally, restoration may be a kind of physical correlate of faith: We make our dead look younger for the same reason that corpses are bedecked in jewels in other cultures—because they must look their best when they enter their "second life" beyond the grave. There is no real contradiction in these beliefs. In a culture where status consciousness and a belief in God are as richly intertwined as in ours, there is nothing inconsistent about perking Uncle Harry up so he looks good to God *and* to his friends.

HEARTS AND FLOWERS:

THE MATING GAME

KISSING

Kissing as a means of expressing affection and sexual interest seems to have developed more elaborately in Western cultures than in Eastern ones. Anthropologists report many instances in which peoples of non-Western societies are mystified or shocked by the practice. Royston Pike (1966) tells the story of the English traveler Winwoode Reade, who in the 1860s offered his lips to a nubile African girl named Ananga and was vehemently repulsed by her: "Ananga knew that the serpent moistens its victim with its lips before it begins its repast. . . . The poor child had thought that I was going to dine off her." The Romans, on the other hand, had already developed kissing to such an art that they had three terms for the custom: *basium* for the kiss between acquaintances, *osculum* for that between close friends, and *suavium* for that between lovers. Our kissing heritage, obviously, comes from Rome.

It is too simple to say, however, that the West kisses and the rest of the planet does not. Havelock Ellis makes a useful distinction between the tactile and the olfactory kiss, suggesting that both varieties, in different ways, may derive from infantile and even animal impulses. In the Western-style tactile kiss, it is the mouth that is the focus of activity. Ellis surmises that behind the desire to press lip to lip are three antecedent instincts: the suckling instinct of the infant, the maternal impulse to lick the young, and the instinct (observable in mammalian mating) for the male to bite the mounted female. In the olfactory kiss, on the other hand, we see a survival of the primitive sniffing instinct. The old joke about Eskimos rubbing noses has, in fact, a sound ethnographic basis, and the Eskimos are not alone in this activity. Numerous people around the world touch not lips, but cheeks or noses, and the biological origin of this may well be the desire to sniff prey, food, or mate as a preliminary testing of the waters.

"X" FOR A KISS

Lovers who sign their letters with a string of "X"s, indicating an equivalent number of kisses, are carrying on a medieval tradition necessitated by almost universal illiteracy. Rudolph Brasch tells us that in the Middle Ages, people who could not sign their names to documents marked them with an "X" instead (in the presence of witnesses) and kissed the mark to affirm their sincerity; "eventually the kiss and the cross became synonymous." The choice of the "X" as a symbol of a personal guarantee was not accidental. The "X"-cross, or *crux decussata,* was sacred to the memory of St. Andrew (the brother of St. Peter), who was crucified on this type of cross. Thus writing and then kissing the "X" was making a pledge in the martyred saint's name. Although this is a feasible explanation, I think it more likely that the kissed "X" pledge owes its origins to the Greek letter "X," or chi, which in church lore always stands for Christ.

WHISTLING AT WOMEN

When feminists call street corner whistlers "animals," they are being more precise than they know. Attempts to attract females by means of vocal signals are quite common among animals. Clellan S. Ford and Frank A. Beach discuss mating calls among a variety of our ancestors, including frogs and toads, alligators, lizards, apes and monkeys, and, of course, birds.

The gecko, a lizard, emits a "chirping" call "to which females respond by approaching the calling individual." Baboons use lip smacking and dental clicking sounds, while male and female howler monkeys produce a sound by vibrating their tongues. "Characteristically," Ford and Beach write, "the individual that is solicited in this fashion responds by producing the same tongue movements, and then the pair copulates." The street corner jerk should be so lucky.

The most common forms of human vocal solicitation these days seem to be baboonlike lip smacking and the even less mistakable and less imaginative statement of intent: "Hey, baby, how'd you like to get it on?" The old-fashioned, rising and falling (and misnamed) "wolf whistle" (no wolf or other canine emits a whistle) is still practiced by aging roués, and it serves as audible evidence that human evolution still has a long way to go.

FLIRTING

The word *flirt* entered the English language in the sixteenth century, when it approximated *flit,* meaning to dart from one thing to another. Used as a noun, a flirt was an "inconstant" person, generally a woman, characterized variously (according to the *Oxford English Dictionary*) as "a pert, young hussy," a woman of "loose character," or one who "plays at courtship." Today the sense is less meretricious, but the underlying notion of inconstancy remains. This is appropriate, for what we mean by flirting, which can be engaged in by a man or a woman, is, by its biological nature, evidence of uncertainty or instability. The female courtship play that involves eye-fluttering, hands in front of the mouth, hesitant smiles, and furtive inviting glances registers not so much the "cock-teasing" that frustrated Casanovas take it for, but rather a quite logical ambivalence: the uncertainty of a potential sexual partner regarding a potentially dangerous man.

Irenäus Eibl-Eibesfeldt relates such behavior, in fact, to the primordial "flight or fight" response—the common behavioral response among animals when they are in a threatening situation. As an example of the cross-cultural ubiquity of flirting behavior, he points to the face-hiding signal, a sign that is at once a show of embarrassment and a come-on. It is observable not only in the "liberated" countries of the West but also among Samoans, Balinese, Africans, Papuans, and Waika Indians.

SPIN THE BOTTLE

Kissing games such as Flashlight, Post Office, and Spin the Bottle have been popular in American culture for centuries. One explanation is that such potentially erotic entertainments provide the sexually awakening adolescent an outlet for physical desires. But psychologist Brian Sutton-Smith contends that they play a more subtle function. Spin the Bottle, in which a youngster must kiss the person to whom a spun bottle points, is one of the most popular kissing games because it regulates and depersonalizes, rather than enhances, real intimacy. Such games, which are played by unsophisticated and tongue-tied young teenagers, provide a "bridge function," introducing players to adult activities without requiring significant risk-taking or commitment. The chance element of Spin the Bottle allows contact beyond personal choice or responsibility: "I couldn't help it; I *had* to kiss her."

Even when chance is not a strong feature, the obligatory nature of kissing games serves as a crisis management device, both enabling and restricting experiment. As "adventures of a non-hazardous kind," such games "provide a guarantee of certain gratification, in this case relationship with the opposite sex, but they place limitations on excess." It is precisely these limitations that make them popular.

PARKING

Back in the pre-pill 1950s, when sexual mores were more constrained than they are today, it used to be a joke among teenagers that the baby boom owed a lot to Detroit. But the roadside rendezvous was only abetted, not created, by the advent of the automobile. William Fielding says that roadside kissing was practiced in horse and buggy days—and not only by the equestrian-minded.

As for the term *parking* itself, Eric Partridge (1983) says it is mid-century American. The term's immediate antecedents, necking and petting, frequently combined with it in the 1950s, come from the 1920s and are also American. The older antecedent "spooning" is English, from the 1830s, when it meant lovemaking in general, especially of a sentimental kind. An American, and potentially more carnal, interpretation of the term appeared in the 1860s, when "spooning" meant lying close together, in the manner of nested utensils.

DUTCH TREAT

To go Dutch treat, or simply "go Dutch," means to share the expenses of a social engagement.

Eric Partridge identifies *Dutch treat* as a late-nineteenth-century term, and he speaks of Dutch lunches and Dutch suppers as potluck affairs where everyone contributes. But the linking of the Dutch with things that shouldn't be done—and specifically with cheapness and sham—goes back to the seventeenth century, when the Dutch and the English were mercantile and military rivals. According to Partridge, a "Dutch bargain" at that time was an uneven, one-sided deal; "Dutch reckoning" was an unitemized account; and "Dutch widow" was slang for harlot. Later centuries brought in "Dutch courage," for bravery induced by drink; "Dutch concert," for discordant music; "Dutch nightingale," meaning a frog; and "double Dutch," for gibberish. So to split expenses with a female was to behave, according to the cavaliers of our mother country, like those peculiar and suspicious folk across the Channel.

CHAPERONS

The original literal meaning of the term *chaperon* was "little cape," and it referred to a hood worn by nobles from about the fourteenth century on. It acquired the connotation of "protectress" in the early eighteenth century because, as the *Oxford English Dictionary* explains, the human chaperon "shelters the youthful debutante as a hood shelters the face."

Chaperons are usually enlisted today to maintain decorum and prevent mischief among teenagers, particularly at high school social functions; their interest seems as much in protecting property as in inhibiting amorous adventures. Until a generation ago, however, the chaperon's role was more precise: It was to protect the reputation of good families by ensuring that their most valued pieces of property, their nubile daughters, were not compromised by gentleman callers. Specifically this meant constant attendance, everywhere from the park to the parlor; in terms of tact and tactics, it frequently meant not so much physically separating the two panting young bodies, but, in Emily Post's delicate phrasing, "making Pamela aware of Heppy Heel's worthlessness." Thus the chaperon system—whether managed by the Spanish *duenna,* the Victorian maiden aunt, or the American grown-up "pal"—was an expression of the cult of virginity. In a roundabout way it may have served as a kind of birth control for unmarried members of the upper classes. It may not be accidental that it reached its peak before the wide use of the condom or that it faded out with the advent of the pill.

DINNER, THEN BED

Women often complain that men who have taken them out to dinner also expect to take them home to bed, as if the price of the meal had to be repaid with sexual favors. Looked at as an economic transaction, such an arrangement is distasteful; yet the exchange can be put in a broader perspective. The metaphoric connection between eating and sex is registered in many catch phrases; think, for example, of "flesh," "tasty," "licking my lips," "piece of meat," and "good enough to eat." It is this symbolic connection, I believe, and not the monetary element, that makes "bed after dinner" a predictable gaucherie. The marriage feast is only the most obvious example of the link between eating and sex. In numerous cultures, from ancient times to the present, the bride and groom's consumption of a common meal is the visible sign that they are now "one body." Marston Bates has suggested a bond of analogy between bed and board. Put simply, this means that we generally do not have sexual relations with those we would not dine with. The romantic dinner may be, not an entrapment of the woman, but an encoded sexual act in itself. As the movie *Tom Jones* made uproariously clear back in 1963, it is more than a mere linguistic accident that the words *carnivore* and *carnal* are related.

THE MISSIONARY POSITION

With very rare exceptions among monkeys, human beings are the only mammals that engage in sexual intercourse face to face. The popularity of ventral (as opposed to dorsal) intercourse may derive from the greater clitoral stimulation involved. This position is the favored one in a wide range of traditional societies, as well as, of course, in our own.

But there is a distinction to be drawn between the ventral lovemaking position in general and the specific form of that position that is preferred in the Anglo-American West. The Kinsey reports of the late forties and early fifties described a number of variant positions that were known to American lovers—ventral, dorsal, and lateral positions—yet pointed out that the preferred position among two-thirds of their sample was the "male dominant" one in which the woman lies on her back and the man lies directly on top of her. Even after the hullabaloo of the 1970s women's movement, Shere Hite reported that among the women she had interviewed, this was still the most common position.

It is this male-on-top, belly-to-belly position, and not face-to-face copulation in general, that is often referred to as the missionary position. Eric Partridge says that the phrase arose among English-speaking Pacific Islanders as a contemptuous description of the one position that nineteenth-century preachers permitted in the copulatory repertoire. Their suspicion of other positions derived from a suspicion of pleasure itself (particularly female pleasure) and tied in nicely with the patriarchal notion that a woman's task in lovemaking was purely passive: She was to lie still and "take" it.

The South Seas natives found this idea ridiculous. Bronislaw Malinowski reported that among Melanesians the preferred position was for the man to kneel between the woman's outspread legs and to pull her pelvis up to his. This was a face-to-face position that provided much more opportunity for mutual movement than was provided by the missionaries' choice. Melanesian natives amused themselves by mimicking the rigidity of Western lovemaking. They described the belly-to-belly position in this way: "The man overlies heavily the woman; he presses her heavily downwards, she cannot respond." Which was precisely the point.

ASKING FOR A WOMAN'S HAND

Ernest Crawley showed that in many cultures the joining of hands is "a ceremonial pre-representation of the actual union in marriage, assisting that union by making it safe and by making it previously, and as it were objectively." The tradition of a man asking for a woman's hand is also related specifically to a Roman marriage custom, the *dextrarum junctio* ("joining of right hands"), in which a bride was "handed over" from father to husband. This was part of a ceremony called *coemptio,* a kind of mock purchase in which the groom-to-be gave the father a coin and he "manumitted" or released his daughter from his *manus* ("hand") and transferred her to the *manus* of her husband. In the Roman civil ceremony of manumission ("letting go of the hand"), a slaveowner emancipated one of his possessions. An equivalent "letting go" can be seen in *coemptio* and in modern marriage ceremonies where a father gives the bride away.

PROPOSING ON BENDED KNEE

The tradition of proposing marriage from a kneeling position is a curious one considering that kneeling typically indicates abasement and that in the majority of marriages, even today, it is seldom the man who is abased. There are probably vestiges of chivalry involved here. Knights in the service of a lady would frequently display their readiness to be commanded by dipping the knee in the mistress's presence. And in both the modern and the medieval gestures, the same formal dissimulation is at work. The presentation of one's husbandly "services" on the knee should be seen as the formulaic validation of a necessary fiction: the idea that in spite of their economic and political powerlessness, it is really women who control social affairs. This is another example of the pedestal ploy, that modern version of chivalry that keeps women subservient by making them the willing victims of male "esteem" (see LADIES FIRST).

ENGAGEMENT RING

The wedding ring signifies union. The engagement ring, which is believed to have preceded it in history, signifies only the *promise* of union. Appropriately it is also called a betrothal ring, since it implies the troth, or good faith, of the man and woman to go through with the marriage vows. In ancient times, rings were used commonly as pledges of a bargain, and they have survived as tokens of fidelity even into these days of written contracts. T. S. Knowlson recounted a medieval custom in which a broken piece of gold was used in troth-plighting. The bride- and groom-to-be would each keep half as a mutual promise to be married. The exchange of gold rings was a later medieval development, comfortably assimilated into the ancient bargain-sealing tradition. According to Marcia Seligson, the popularity of diamonds came in even later than that. The Austrian archduke Maximilian presented the first notable betrothal rock to his French fiancée, Mary of Burgundy, in the fifteenth century. Diamonds became universally accepted as engagement stones only in the last century (see DIAMONDS).

DIAMONDS

Diamonds are appreciated less for their scarcity than for their traditional, symbolic appeal. This appeal derives from two peculiarities of the stones. The first is hardness. The diamond is acknowledged to be the hardest substance in nature. Though all this means is that it is impervious to surface scratching (it can be broken quite easily), this attribute has given it an aura of imperishability. The Roman writer Pliny even claimed that you could hit a diamond with a hammer and break the tool. Obviously he never tried it, for the diamond would have shattered into dust. Yet, on the strength of the legend, the diamond remains a symbol of imperishable love.

The second quality that makes the diamond so desirable is its ability, when it is properly faceted, to play with light. Cut diamonds display not only "brilliance," which is the jeweler's term for reflected light, but also an internal "fire." This internal light play has come to symbolize the "fires" of love.

The use of the diamond as a romance-enhancer is a relatively recent development. George Blakey tells us that until the mid-fifteenth century, the diamond symbolized not love but royal power. When Agnes Sorel, mistress of King Charles VII of France, began wearing diamonds, they started to take on their current romantic connotation, as well as a parallel "slightly risqué image."

It was this romantic and risqué image that accompanied the stone into the late nineteenth century, when the discovery of diamonds in South Africa led to a marketing revolution. For centuries diamonds had been worn only by the wealthy. Then, in the 1880s, Cecil Rhodes established the mining and distribution operation that came to be known as De Beers, and the stones gradually became a mass commodity. The De Beers company, which once controlled 95 percent of the diamond trade, still monopolizes the marketing of the finest stones and has done an enviable job of linking these bits of carbon with the idea of eternal love. It was De Beers that gave us those pictures of moony couples over the caption "A Diamond Is Forever." Today, whether she's an heiress or a shop girl, the bride-to-be wants only one thing on her finger as an emblem of undying affection—and three out of four get it. Cecil Rhodes would be proud.

BANNS OF MARRIAGE

Catholic canon law, for both the Western and Eastern rites, stipulates that an impending marriage of parishioners must be announced publicly three times before the wedding takes place. This custom, which is almost a thousand years old, is called reading (or posting) the banns, from the Middle English term *ban* or *bane,* meaning a proclamation or announcement. The purpose of the banns is to provide protection against improper marriages, by giving the congregation an opportunity to object—say, on the grounds that one of the betrothed is already married or is known to be a follower of Satan. Technically, the banns must be announced on three successive Sundays or on three successive days of obligation (Sundays included), and the marriage cannot take place until three days after the final announcement.

WEDDING INVITATIONS

To judge from the etiquette books, sending out wedding invitations
is a procedure only slightly less fraught with hazards than disman-
tling a booby-trapped bomb. I have yet to see a manual that devotes
less than a dozen pages to the custom's intricacies. When it comes
to major puzzles like the "double wedding of cousins" and the "girl
with the same name as her mother" the authorities naturally diverge:
But there is one thing on which they all agree, and that is that those
who are giving the bride away make must their preeminence clear
at the outset by putting the invitation in their names and by stating
that "your presence is requested" at the marriage of their so-and-so.
Thus: "Col. and Mrs. Reginald Macao request your presence at the
marriage of their daughter Elsie" (Elsie gets her own line here) "to
Mr. Gaylord Lucid Bonbon." Notice that Gaylord comes last. The
wedding is the bride's affair, done up by the bride's people; it is only
happening *to* the groom.

The "bride first" convention is not accidental. It is the inevitable
formal structure of a marital system that derives from marriage by
arrangement and purchase—a system in which the father (or other
"giver") owns the bride and must make a public announcement that
he is surrendering control over her before anyone will come to the
wedding. No such announcement must be made for the groom (Gaylord's parents have zip to do with the invitations) because of the tacit
assumption that Gaylord can make his own decisions; he need not
be offered (or freed) by his folks. The fact that the bride's people
typically pay for the wedding, therefore, is not the real reason that
they issue the invitation. The real reason is social decorum. If Reginald and Mrs. Macao did not formally invite, Elsie would have to
elope.

Of course, there is change in the wind. Some invitations today are
issued jointly by the bride and the groom. I don't know what Amy
Vanderbilt would say about this, but I consider it dangerously sub-
versive. Once daughters start announcing that they are not the mere
property of their parents, what freedoms will they claim next?

BRIDAL SHOWERS

The bridal shower is generally considered to be a survivor of the dowry system. As Lillian Eichler tells the oft-repeated tale, centuries ago a young Dutch miller fell in love with a girl who returned his affections, and all might have been well had he not been as generous as he was smitten. In the habit of donating his bread to the needy, he had become poor himself; so the girl's father blocked the wedding by withholding her dowry, and urged her to marry a rich farmer. The local townspeople, hearing of the couple's plight, "showered" the daughter with so many household goods that she soon had a much larger dowry than her father himself had provided. The two were promptly betrothed.

Apocryphal or not, the story indicates the communal and spontaneous nature of the bridal shower. Typically showers are given by and for close friends of the bride, and the shower gifts that etiquette recommends are conventionally of the domestic variety. In fact, invitations often specify "linen shower" or "kitchen shower." Also, shower gifts are supposed to be relatively inexpensive—that is, in comparison with wedding gifts.

STAG PARTIES

Bachelor gatherings before weddings are quite common, and there is no great mystery why: Young single men about to lose a crony naturally want to bid him farewell. It's the nature of the goodbye that is interesting, and this varies from culture to culture. According to William Fielding, the prewedding bachelor dinner originated in Sparta, where it was called a "men's mess." He gives no details about the activities that took place, but judging from Spartan life in general, they probably ran to muscle-flexing and brawls. In Europe and England a traditional stag-party custom was for the party to drink a toast to the bride and then smash their glasses in unison so that, according to ancient custom, they could never be used for a lesser purpose. In America the prewedding party tends toward boisterousness and blue movies, which is very likely an outgrowth of the fact that they took their present shape on the frontier, where—as a Midwestern comic once quipped—the women were scarce and the sheep were nervous. The terms *stag party, stag dinner,* and *stag dance* all come from the nineteenth-century West. The current emphasis on getting the groom drunk and regaling him with off-color humor is probably the legacy of lonesome miners' makeshift shindigs.

VIRGIN BRIDES

The low point in the status of virginity probably was reached in the early 1970s, when the popular media portrayed constant copulation as the natural state of humankind and bumper stickers and buttons displayed the prurient legend "Virginity is curable." Since then, the spread of AIDS, herpes, and other venereal diseases has done much to restore virginity to its historical place of esteem. Even if we sophisticated Americans frown on hanging the bloody bed linen out of a window after the wedding night (as is still done in Mediterranean hinterlands), there seems little doubt that the idea of the virgin bride is coming back into vogue. In 1981 Barry Tarshis reported that 41 percent of American girls said they wanted to be virgins on their wedding night, and a predictably lower but still significant 20 percent of males agreed that it was a good idea—for their brides.

Feminists frequently point to the idea of virginity for brides but not necessarily for grooms as an example of the sexist double standard. No argument there, but it's worthwhile to note that this dichotomy originated from a socially functional, not merely chauvinistic, bias. The *New Catholic Encyclopedia,* while acknowledging that virginity may be "attributed" to men as well as women, says that it has been historically more "highly honored" in women not only on the grounds of simple virtue but also because "the purity of blood lines and the authenticity of family relationships depend more upon the virtue of the woman than of the man." In other words, there's a pragmatic, economic reason for enforcing chastity on unmarried girls. Only by knowing that his bride is a virgin on their wedding night can a man be certain that the child she later bears is in fact his child. Thus, when a girl insists on saving herself for marriage, what she is really saving is not so much her own purity as the honor of her husband's family name.

JUNE WEDDINGS

The preference for weddings in June may derive from an instinctive human urge that corresponds to the spring rut of animals. The trouble with this Darwinian logic is that even supposing that early hominids displayed the estrus cycle of other animals (a debatable assumption), June is pretty late for such pairing.

The secret of the month's propitiousness is that Juno was the Roman goddess of marriage. It is because she presided over the sixth month of the Julian calendar that it was considered lucky for weddings. May, on the other hand, was considered unlucky—a bizarre superstition, since Maia was a fruition goddess, but one that sheds light on the tendency to wait until June.

In the survival of the pagan custom, inertia has certainly played a part, but so have common sense and the desire for comfort. Mrs. John Sherwood, a commentator on Gilded Age propriety, allowed as how there is "something exquisitely poetical in the idea of a June wedding. It is the very month for the softer emotions and for the wedding journey." The journey was and is the determining consideration. Since the wedding was typically followed by a honeymoon (see HONEYMOON), couples naturally preferred to set the date at the beginning of warm weather, which was also the beginning of the summer vacation season. One does not look forward to Niagara Falls in December.

WHY THE GROOM CAN'T SEE THE BRIDE

It's long been considered bad luck for a groom to see his bride before the ceremony on the wedding day. One explanation for this superstition is that waiting at the altar, wondering how she will look, heightens the drama and lessens the groom's chances of getting cold feet. The sudden appearance of his beloved, decked out like a vision in white, so astonishes the man that he's a husband before he knows what's hit him. The surprise factor thus ensures groomly compliance.

A more substantial historical explanation is that the prohibition is a holdover from primitive seclusion rites, which stipulate that *nobody* should see a betrothed girl before she has passed fully into womanhood. As one of the most significant rites of passage, marriage involves, in Arnold Van Gennep's classic description, a period of separation from old ways, a period of transition, and a period of incorporation into the new. The middle period, a kind of limbo state, is fraught with confusion and imagined perils. In many cultures brides-to-be are considered unclean and are secluded for a period of time before the ceremony so that they will not contaminate others. Whether or not an echo of this attitude plays a role in the modern superstition, it's clear that keeping the bride at a distance until the critical moment reflects the primitive anxiety about transition—the concern that, until the incorporation ceremonies are completed, something can always go wrong.

WEDDING ATTENDANTS

The typical American wedding includes a bridal party composed of, in addition to the happy couple, a best man, a maid or matron of honor, and equal numbers of ushers and bridesmaids. There are several plausible explanations for this gaggle of attendants. The most obvious and most mundane one is that the wedding party is enlisted to facilitate matters, to emotionally and physically support the bride and groom on one of the most trying days of their lives, and to see to it that the many small details of the ceremony are not botched or ignored. Emily Post calls the best man the "expressman" of the ceremony, charged with "moving things along smoothly," and Barbara Tober observes that the bridesmaids, in the days when many brides were mere children, were called upon to assist her with dressing and with the logistics of moving to her new home.

Among the more exotic explanations for the tradition, the most tenacious has been the idea that the attendants are the modern version of rival war parties, from the days of marriage by capture. Ushers have thus evolved from the groom's men (indeed, ushers used to be called groomsmen) and bridesmaids from the bride's defenders; the best man plays the role of just that—the groom's strongest and most reliable supporter. Champions of the "marriage by capture" thesis fail to explain why the bride's defenders, surely originally male, should have changed gender over the centuries. According to a second theory that makes the party a group of witnesses rather than warriors, bridesmaids and ushers are the modern equivalent of the Roman *advocati,* who stood by the couple to attest to their character and to the validity of the union. A third and most intriguing theory sees the attendants as substitutes for the bride and groom. In the days when evil spirits were thought to be a potential threat to any ceremony, a married couple dressed its friends in costumes identical or similar to their own, to confuse the demons. Nearly identical dressing was common into Victorian times. If the bride stands out dramatically from her bridesmaids today, if may be because we have ceased to be worried about demons.

FLOWERS AND FLOWER GIRLS

Flowers have a mixed symbolism in weddings. On the one hand, because they are light and easily broken, they may symbolize the fragility of virginity. On the other hand, because they testify to fruit-bearing in nature, they can be seen as an emblem of pregnancy and the end of virginity. Early bridal bouquets, Barbara Tober notes, were often made of herbs rather than flowers; among the most popular was dill, which was eaten after the ceremony to "provoke lust." In Tudor England, marigolds were carried, and then eaten, for such a supposed aphrodisiac effect.

The paradox inherent in the symbolism of the flower is made doubly apparent when the flowers are carried or strewn by female children. Today's flower girl harks back to the weddings of medieval times. It was the custom then for two young girls, preferably sisters, to walk before the bride and groom carrying wheat sheaves, a symbol of fruition since the Roman era. Perhaps the flower girl, then as now, helped the adults to manage the tensions of the ceremony. Since marriage was a hazardous as well as a joyous proposition (especially in the days of puerperal fever), having young virgins care for the fertility symbols may have been a way to mute their potentially destructive potency. The presence of the youngster sent a symbolic appeal to the gods: "Look kindly on our lust *and* our innocence."

GIVING THE BRIDE AWAY

Throughout much of human history, brides were sold, not given, to their husbands, and almost certainly it is marriage by purchase that lies behind the custom of giving the bride away. The purchase aspect is not evident from the terminology, but that is due to linguistic disguise; this choice of word reflects the same masquerade that goes on when the phone company promises to "give" you good service.

In many societies women are still sold to their husbands, and it was not that long ago, in enlightened England, that some husbands thought they could even be resold, rather than divorced. T. S. Knowlson, writing of England in the 1880s, reported "at least a dozen cases" of wife-selling—one in which the woman was handed over for "eighteen pence and a glass of beer." Such extreme commercialization of the marriage compact, as Lewis Hyde has pointed out, is a perversion of the very concept of giving. It is too simple, he says, to say that the woman given in marriage is property: She is a "special kind of property" that is to be confused neither with "chattel" nor with "commodity." As Hyde puts it, "Her father may be able to give her away, but he may not sell her," because as his child she is a gift of God and may only be bestowed on another in the same manner in which she was "received"—that is, without cash or other "consideration." Hyde's elegant essay would be more convincing on this point if parents gave away their sons as well as their daughters.

ALL DRESSED IN WHITE

Marcia Seligson calls the wedding dress the "key metaphor" in the elaborate effort to make the American wedding an "idealized departure from reality," and notes that in the early 1970s, at a time when love-ins, live-ins, and hippie weddings were throwing brickbats at tradition, 94 percent of American brides still chose to be married in white. The color has long been associated with weddings because of its supposed symbolic link to virginity. Commenting slyly on the tradition, Judith Martin (1982) observes that an engaged couple needs to decide "whether wearing a white wedding dress will be worth enduring the sneers of people who believe these must be accessorized by intact hymens."

Viewed historically, the link between white and virginity (or, as it is sometimes euphemized, purity) is not as absolute as is often supposed. Brides in ancient Rome married in white, but because the color signified joy; they were veiled in a bright orange veil, or *flammeum,* that suggested the flames of passion. In the western Catholic tradition, too, white has always been the color of joy, and it remains the iconographically correct hue for such jubilant occasions as Easter Sunday. Some traditional societies use white to denote the significance of various passage ceremonies, among them funerals as well as weddings. For example, among the Andaman Islanders, said A.R. Radcliffe-Brown, white indicated simply a change of status; and the traditional Chinese white for funerals was a symbolic representation of hope.

The "traditional" white wedding dress, moreover, is a recent innovation. Barbara Tober explains that its popularity may owe less to the mystique of virginity than to a curious twist of conspicuous display. Most Victorian brides, she says, wore simply their "best finery" on their wedding day, and many wore traditional ethnic costumes. The white dress was an ostentatiously impractical innovation that became popular among the upper classes precisely because of its defects: "Victorian brides from privileged backgrounds wore white to indicate that they were rich enough to wear a dress for one day only." And throughout the first years of this century, brides from somewhat less privileged backgrounds would trot out the white dress on special occasions throughout the first year of their marriage. The custom of locking the treasure away after the wedding—so that, like a toasting glass, it could never be used for a lesser purpose—is less than a hundred years old.

HOPE CHESTS AND TROUSSEAUS

Today the term *hope chest* is largely metaphoric, and *trousseau* usually means a bridal wardrobe. In the Middle Ages, both terms had broader meanings. *Trousseau* in French means "little bundle," and it referred to a bundle of clothes and linen that a bride took with her to her husband's house. The hope chest was an actual wooden chest, often made by the bride's father in her childhood and filled, item by item, as she grew up. Girls would begin to hand-fashion pieces for their hope chests, including the trousseau items, as soon as they learned how to work a needle. The idea was that a female's reality began only when she became someone's wife. Everything up to the wedding day was fantasy and delayed gratification: Real Life lay, with Hope, in the chest, along with the petit-point napkins and the nuptial nighty.

There was an economic as well as a romantic side to all of this. The contents of the hope chest were a kind of dowry and in some cases, Fielding said, they may have been the dowry itself. In early medieval times, serious suitors had the right to examine the trousseau in detail before proposing. Since the "bundle" might contain not just clothing but also household items such as silver and china, it could provide a fairly accurate measure of the girl's worth. At a time when a marriage without a dowry was unthinkable, the suitor's interest would have been strongly influenced by the value of the girl's possessions.

THE BRIDAL VEIL

Most explanations of the bridal veil fail to distinguish between the temporary, diaphanous veil of modern ceremonies and the permanent, opaque covering of traditional (especially Muslim) societies. There is a superficial connection between the two, and it may be, as feminist anthropologists have observed, that the modern wedding veil, no less than the Iranian *chadoor,* signifies the imposed seclusion and inferiority of women. In Muslim and Hindu societies, the veil and purdah symbolize the separation of the sexes that must be enforced because one sex (the female) is considered dangerous (that is, tempting) to the other. Rudolph Brasch, linking the submissive and separative implications of the custom to the sense of allure that is provided by partial concealment, says that the veil indicates "a woman's original complete submission to her husband," and yet also enhances rather than disguises her attraction, because "hidden goods tend to appear more precious and attractive than those openly on display."

The only objection I would raise to this interpretation is that it fails to take into account that at the conclusion of many modern wedding ceremonies, the husband publicly unveils his wife, and that after the wedding, the veil is never used again. An interpretation that explains this temporary aspect of the veil would focus on the ceremony as a period of intense peril—a transition from one stage of life to another that, among moderns no less than among primitives, must be ringed about with ritual precautions. The modern veil may have less to do with the *chadoor* than with the Jewish wedding canopy, the Anglo-Saxon "care cloth," and the Chinese marital umbrella, all of which guard the couple from baneful influences.

SOMETHING OLD, SOMETHING NEW . . .

The traditional wedding costume should contain, according to an anonymous couplet, "something old, something new, something borrowed, and something blue." The old and the new are not hard to understand: They symbolize, jointly, the passage from the old, unmarried state to that of marital union, and they may also serve to reassure the happy youngsters that their contentment will last into old age. The stipulation of something borrowed, it seems likely, is a method of socializing the ceremony, of demonstrating, by the wearing of something not owned by the couple, that there is community participation in, and approval of, the wedding. (This is the reason, of course, that weddings are public in the first place.) The blue may—I emphasize *may*—be a survivor from Hebrew tradition. According to William Fielding, brides in ancient Israel wore a ribbon of blue on their wedding garments because it was the color of "purity, love, and fidelity." Yet at least one authority on Jewish marriage, Maurice Lamm, specifically denies the connection. Among traditional Jews, he says, the preferred costume color is white.

BOUQUETS AND GARTERS

Since flowers have always symbolized new life, the custom of the bride tossing her bouquet to the assembled single women after the ceremony almost certainly derives from primitive fertility rites, laced with a healthy portion of sympathetic magic. The original ritual very likely had the newly "deflowered" bride throw the symbol of her altered status to a congregation of virgins, so that her good fortune, and the increase of the tribe, might be passed on. The bride's garter is the male version of the bouquet, a symbol of masculine control that can be loosened only by the husband and that symbolizes her sexual fealty to him just as the bouquet symbolizes her promise to bear his children.

As for the evolution of the garter custom, the first step was an English "stocking flinging" ritual in which wedding guests invaded the bridal chamber, tore off the couple's stockings (women guests took off the groom's, male guests the bride's), and hurled them haphazardly around the room. The person whose missile landed on the bride's or groom's nose would, it was supposed, be the next to marry. Gradually this custom was replaced by an even less decorous one: Guests would rush the bride at the altar, to secure one of her garters. As a means of self-preservation, brides eventually removed the garters themselves, tossing them before they could be torn. The modern development, in which the husband removes the precious talisman and keeps it for himself, is a final step away from mob frenzy and toward the couple's personal control.

WEDDING BANDS

Rings have been tokens of loyalty and affection since ancient times, and the incurious leave it at that. Seeing the circle as an emblem of continuity, they take the simple, unbroken wedding band as the representation of undying love.

Those who see marriage as oppression tend to take a more jaundiced view. Typical is Marcia Seligson's suggestion that the wedding ring, reflecting marriage by capture, symbolizes the "rope tied around the woman's waist or wrist and ankles, to subdue her"; other analysts have seen the wedding ring as a miniaturized slave bracelet. Dyspeptic as such comments may seem, they cannot be dismissed out of hand. Etymology gives credence to the argument, since wedding rings are typically called bands, and the first meaning of *band* in the *Oxford English Dictionary* is "anything with which one's body or limbs are bound, in restraint of personal liberty."

As for the "third finger, left hand" tradition, this too has both a romantic and a more mundane explanation. Greek anatomical theory saw this finger connected by a special vein to the heart, and so it was the appropriate digit to be "bound" in romantic attachment. Seligson and others report that the left hand is the hand of subjection; thus the placement of the ring on this hand might signify the submission of the wife to her husband. There is also considerable anthropological speculation that makes the left the side of weakness and subjection. In his classic essay on the right hand, Robert Hertz claimed that the wedding ring is a protective device, needed by the "exposed and defenseless" left side: "The ring that we wear on the third finger of the left hand is intended primarily to keep temptations and other bad things from us."

Such symbolic interpretations are provocative, but there may be a simpler explanation. The third finger of the left hand, for most people, is the least used of all the ten digits, and in addition the third fingers are the only fingers that cannot be extended easily. Making the third finger of the left hand the ring finger, therefore, might have had a quite practical basis: A ring on that finger would last longer, because it would be less likely to be battered about.

GOLD

Judged on the traditional economic grounds of rarity and utility, gold is now and always has been incredibly overpriced. To appreciate why "real" jewelry, including wedding and engagement bands, must be made of gold, you have to consider what I call the El Dorado Factor—that blend of avarice, wish fulfillment, and awe that has always given the metal an irrational, magical aura. Makers of wedding rings like the metal partly because it does not tarnish and partly because it is easy to work, at least when mixed with harder alloys. But to these utilitarian considerations must be added a much older, quasi-aesthetic consideration: Gold is symbolically, not just physically, imperishable—and people have seen it that way for so long that no amount of new data can change the perception. Platinum and iridium, for example, are both rarer and more useful than gold, yet no one uses them for wedding rings. The only thing that might have altered the tradition would have been the discovery of iridium in King Tut's tomb.

CRYING AT WEDDINGS

Marcia Seligson claims that, by her "informal tally" of American wedding ceremonies, "80 percent of all wedding guests choke up." This seemingly inappropriate response—the display of a distress signal at a joyous event—is a common one throughout human cultures. Edward Westermarck noted that a "ceremonial reluctance or crying of the bride is found among all Indo-European peoples." He dismisses the predictable explanation that the practice is a survival of marriage by capture, and suggests instead that it was related to "coyness or sexual modesty, real or assumed." A cogent argument, but it does not really explain very well why in our culture it is the guests, far more often than the bride, who are expected to be streaked with tears. A. R. Radcliffe-Brown, commenting on the non-European culture of the Andaman Islanders, provided a hint in the right direction. Ceremonial weeping, he wrote, serves to cement social bonds that are threatened by pivotal events like weddings and, of course, funerals. The formalized emotional display at such functions (whether they are happy or sad functions) unites the participants in common cause at precisely that (dangerous) moment when a change of state occurs—when we are in the midst of an uncertain rite of passage. So a ceremonial distress display, far from being out of place at a wedding, is an appropriate register of perceived instability: By crying, the guests are saying to one another and to the couple, "Let's hope everybody gets *through* this all right."

KISSING THE BRIDE

Western brides have been kissed as part of the wedding ceremony since the days of the Roman empire. Among engaged Roman couples, the kiss was a legal bond, the public certification that the union had taken place symbolically; if one of the contracting parties died before the formal ceremony, the survivor could keep the wedding gifts if, and only if, the two had kissed. "The symbolic value of this kiss," Nicolas Perella notes, "depends upon the deeply rooted idea of the kiss as a vehicle for the transference of power or 'souls.' " The kiss as a binding symbol survives in the modern wedding ceremony. According to the church and the state, a couple is one when the officiant pronounces them so, but that is never enough for the guests: The community sees the ceremony as completed—that is, as formally "sealed"—only when the bride and groom kiss.

The wedding kiss also symbolizes the change of state of the bride. When he lifts her veil to touch her lips, the husband announces to the congregation that he defines and accepts her new identity. Just as the kiss of the Prince awakens Sleeping Beauty, so the kiss of her own Prince Charming fractures the bride's slumber of maidenhood and initiates her into adult life. The custom of having the guests kiss the bride may be seen as an elaboration of this initiation motif. The serial pecking ritual that often follows the ceremony—in which everybody from Uncle Joe to the newspaper boy gets a shot at the bride—should be seen not as a harmless sexual game, and much less as the distribution of bridal favors, but as a communal welcoming rite. The guests' kissing fortifies and endorses the husband's.

BRIDAL

It is a longstanding tradition for principals and guests to consume vast quantities of alcohol at wedding receptions, and the term *bridal* reflects this bibulous heritage. Early medieval marriage celebrations in England were even more notoriously drunken than ours are, and the preferred drink in those days was *ealu,* or "ale." The celebration, from at least the eleventh century on, was known as the *brid-ealu,* or "bride ale," referring to the ale that was drunk to the bride's honor. The literal meaning began to be obscured, by the contraction to *bridal,* sometime in the thirteenth century.

OF RICE AND CAKES

The customs of throwing rice at a wedding, and of eating cake at the reception, both hark back to Roman times. Roman brides were married holding wheat sheaves, and with their new husbands they ate a postceremonial cake made of wheat. The Latin term for such a wedding, in fact, was *conferreatio,* meaning "eating wheat together." Rice-throwing is an outgrowth of the wheat sheaves, and the wedding cake ultimately of the conferration.

I say "ultimately" because the wheat sheave and wheat cake traditions, both of them designed to ensure fertility by sympathetic magic, diverged in the first century A.D. The conferration was momentarily forgotten, and medieval brides had to be contented with the sheaves, either carried or worn as a chaplet. Then, sometime during the Middle Ages, Christians borrowed the Jewish custom of throwing handfuls of wheat over married couples, as an incentive to "increase and multiply." The cast wheat was eaten afterward, as a compliment to the bride, and presumably it was because of this practice that the wheat was next baked into cakes. Thus small wedding cakes, or biscuits, came into vogue, with custom stipulating that these small items, just like the earlier loose wheat, be thrown (and usually broken) over the bride's head. Taking no chances, the fertility mongers generally issued such cakes to invited guests.

Edwin Daniel Wolff's whimsical explanation of the final step in the evolution of the rice-throwing custom is as cogent as any: "When wheat-throwing ceased because the grains were baked into cakes the onlookers at a marriage felt a sense of deprivation; they were accustomed to hurling things at the bride and they wanted to continue that pleasant practice." So the uninvited audience, which had not been provided with wheat cakes to toss, chose rice: It symbolized fertility just as well, and it was "white and clean and cheap."

Meanwhile, the folks who had been provided with wheat cakes (that is, the wedding list) continued to hurl them as before. Some of them were eaten by the young couple; some were taken home by hopeful maidens, who would place them under their pillows in the hope of receiving dreams of future husbands; some were distributed to the poor. The remainder were piled together, to be coated with almond paste or sugar. Eventually this pile of coated cakes grew into the modern, tiered creation—the conferration meal back in spades.

CUTTING THE CAKE

The cake-cutting at modern weddings is a four-step comic ritual that sustains masculine prerogatives in the very act of supposedly subverting them. Until early in this century, the bride cut the first slice of cake herself, because of the belief, as Lillian Eichler commented in 1924, that "if anyone else cuts into the cake first, the bride's happiness and prosperity are cut into." Now, in the first step of the comedy, the groom helps direct the bride's hand—a symbolic demonstration of male control that was unnecessary in the days of more tractable women. She accepts this gesture and, as a further proof of submissiveness, performs the second step of the ritual, offering him the first bite of cake, the gustatory equivalent of her body, which he will have the right to "partake of" later. In the third step, the master-servant relationship is temporarily upset, as the bride mischievously pushes the cake into her new husband's face, leaving him with a chin full of icing. Significantly, this act of revolt is performed in a childish fashion, and the groom is able to endure it without losing face because it ironically demonstrates his superiority: His bride is an imp needing supervision. That the bride herself accepts this view of things is demonstrated in the ritual's final step, in which she wipes the goo apologetically from his face. This brings the play back to the beginning, as she is once again obedient to his wiser judgment. Thus the entire tableau may be seen as a dramatization of potential marital tensions and a theatrical resolution of those tensions in favor of the dominance of the male.

THE BRIDE'S FAMILY PAYING FOR THE WEDDING

Since it is traditionally girls and not boys who are taught to look forward to their wedding day as the most important day in life, one might suppose that the bride's family pays the freight that day simply because they're the more interested party: If things are to be perfect for Daddy's little girl, then Daddy had better cover the bets. Could be. But a broader historical explanation would see the wedding bill as an outgrowth of the dowry.

The dowry serves as a kind of "return gift to the bridegroom," according to William Fielding, in societies in which he must purchase his beloved from her father. Arnold Van Gennep notes that the wedding expenses among the Turko-Mongols, as among modern Americans, were typically borne by the bride's family, as part of a "system of compensation" offsetting the *kalym,* or bride price of the girl. Fielding documents the same kind of compensation in ancient Greek and Roman society. The survival of the dowry into modern times is evident, most famously, in Shakespeare's *Taming of the*

Shrew, in which the original attraction of the shrewish bride is that she comes dangling ducats behind her. Since brides are no longer purchased in modern America (at least not openly), the compensatory value of the dowry no longer exists; yet the custom of Kate's dad footing the bill survives.

The word *wedding* means, roughly, "bride price." In early medieval England the *wed* was the earnest money or pledge a bridegroom gave the girl's father. So linguistically, if not in actual practice, when the father of the bride pays for the wedding, he is mirroring an ancient system of marital kickback.

DISPLAYING THE GIFTS

Etiquette columnist Miss Manners, responding to a reader's query about the best way to display wedding gifts, counsels that it is "by putting them to their intended use in the bridal couple's home, for guests to admire or not admire as they wish" (Martin, 1982). She thus reflects a growing consensus that the ancient custom of wedding gift display, far from being an innocent acknowledgment of the couple's good fortune, is a vestige of barbaric ostentation. It's hard to dispute this view, especially when we consider such examples of conspicuous display as the 3,500 gifts presented to the Duke of York and his bride at their 1893 wedding. But there is a broader social benefit to the custom that liberal iconoclasts like Miss Manners fail to appreciate. It's quite true, as she points out, that the only feeling satisfied by gift display is "curiosity about who spent what," but in a highly possessions-oriented, market-driven society such as ours, that feeling is not to be taken lightly. The desire to excel others in purchasing power is a major force behind capitalism. The invidious distinction set up by a public display of goods—at a wedding reception no less than at a Tupperware party or in a department store—may be a psychological *sine qua non* for an economy built on excess.

The display of gifts, therefore, serves somewhat the same function in our society that the potlatch—the lavish display and distribution of excess goods—served in the society of the Northwest Coast Indians: It not only enhances the givers' status, but it validates the self-defining ideals of a people whose identity is strongly involved with ownership.

GIFT REGISTRY

Bridal gift registry allows a couple to receive a myriad of goodies from a single source without the risk of duplication. Barbara Tober says the registry custom began in a Rochester, Minnesota, store called China Hall, back in 1901. Its creator was a young clerk named Herman Winkle, who to help himself keep track of what gifts had and had not been purchased for specific brides, began recording names and patterns on index cards. His idea caught on, first in jewelry stores and then in department stores, in the 1930s, when the Depression made consumer efficiency a necessity for many, and was later picked up by furniture stores, gourmet shops, bookstores, and even the gift shop of the Metropolitan Museum of Art in New York. Gift registries today are often computerized, which makes them even more efficient. There is really no longer any excuse for a bride and groom to be caught in Wedding Hell, staring dolefully at six more pineapple forks than they can use.

"DECORATING" THE WEDDING CAR

The wedding car that trails tin cans, pots and pans, and old shoes is a stock image in old movies. Though the style of decoration has changed, the impulse to "trash the car" still survives: Today's form of the traditional sabotage is the streamer and the "Just Married" sign.

Such affronts to the dignity of the getaway vehicle are vestiges of a medieval folk tradition known as *charivari,* or, in America, *shivaree.* The *Oxford English Dictionary* defines the charivari as "a serenade of 'rough music,' with kettles, pans, tea-trays, and the like, used in France, in mockery and derision of incongruous or unpopular marriages, and of unpopular persons generally." In America the custom was extended to apply to socially acceptable as well as "unpopular" marriages; Mitford Mathews describes the American shivaree as "a noisy demonstration, especially as a serenade for a newly wedded couple."

What this meant, until very recently, was that the newly joined couple's close friends would gather raucously outside their bedroom window, doing their best to intrude on the Magic Moment, until the groom asked them in for a drink. In the jet age, when a married couple's first night together may be spent a continent away from the chapel, well-meaning tormentors have had to settle for attaching their rough music to the fender of the getaway car.

Why anyone would want to torture his or her friends in this way is a bit of a puzzle. Some anthropologists have depicted the shivaree as a surviving exorcism rite, in which evil spirits that might threaten the happy couple are banished by the general pandemonium. This is an appealing theory, but there is a simpler psychological one. Since most rough music makers tend to be the same unmarried males who set up stag parties for the groom-to-be, it is reasonable to assume that their envy of his good fortune plays a part in the good-natured harassment. What we cannot have we frequently mock. The hidden message of the shoes on the car, then, may be this: If I cannot have what you have, I can at least make you look ridiculous. The sexual jealousy implicit here is all the more obvious in the bedroom-window shivaree, where the entire point of the ceremony is to keep the newly marrieds out of bed.

SHOES ON THE CAR

Tin cans make noise and thus provide the clatter that is appropriate to a good trashing of the honeymoon vehicle. The reason for tying old shoes to the fender—still a widespread custom in some quarters—is not so evident. It derives from the older custom of throwing a shoe after the departing couple, which in turn derives from an even older association of the shoe with property transfer. In the ancient Near East, the transfer of a shoe or sandal from seller to buyer symbolized the binding of a transaction: This was the custom among the Hebrews, the Assyrians, and the Egyptians. Among the ancient Anglo-Saxons, moreover, the father of a bride gave one of her shoes to the bridegroom as an indication that authority over her had passed from sire to mate. Significantly, this ceremony was concluded by the husband using the shoe as a mock scepter, tapping his bride on the head with it. So the shoes tied on the fender show that the groom now "owns" his bride. (The Cinderella tale twists the tradition, by making the hard-to-fill slipper the symbol of the Prince's expectation of wedded bliss.)

ELOPEMENT

Modern reasons for elopement—the disapproval of parents and the stress of preparing for a formal wedding—fostered so-called runaway marriages in earlier times as well, although during those long centuries in which marriage was largely a financial arrangement, no doubt problems of exchange also played a part. If, for example, Juliet's parents opposed Romeo's attentions because he lacked a sufficient bride price, the lovers could circumvent opposition by running away; the same recourse could be taken if it were Juliet's portion, the dowry, that was lacking.

In our society, running away is not in itself considered equivalent to marriage, but William Fielding notes that in many societies, this has been precisely the case. Among various American Indian peoples, as well as in parts of Asia, a couple was deemed to be wed if they had fled their homes and lived together in hiding for a recognized period of time. (Cohabitation is occasionally recognized today, by the same logic, as "common law" marriage.) This works, of course, only when the elopement is an escape from parental oversight; it does not apply to flights into adultery. Interestingly, this is a fairly recent distinction. Well into the nineteenth century, according to the *Oxford English Dictionary,* the principal legal meaning of *elope* was for a wife "to run away from her husband in the company of a paramour."

THE HONEYMOON

Popular etymology places the honeymoon originally in Germany or Scandinavia. It is supposed to have been the month, or "moon," following a Teutonic marriage, when the bride and groom would retreat to a secluded spot and partake of the honeyed wine called mead, thought to have aphrodisiac properties. The ancient people of northern Europe did drink mead, or metheglin, and they may have gone into seclusion after marriage, but the idea of a honeymoon, or honeymonth, among them is pure conjecture, and apparently a fairly recent one. The *Oxford English Dictionary,* whose editors love to relate (and debunk) interpretations of this sort, don't give it even a nod, suggesting strongly that the explanation was not current until the nineteenth century. The first printed reference to the term *honeymoon,* moreover, does not appear until 1546: The supposedly earlier *honeymonth* doesn't come in until a century and a half after that, and it isn't until the early 1800s that *honeymoon* is found referring to the journey that the couple takes after their wedding. The original (that is, sixteenth-century) term, the *Oxford English Dictionary* concludes, referred not to the period of a month, but to the changeable nature of the moon itself: Newly marrieds are in the "honey," or full phase of their love, which, like the moon, is bound someday to wane. The nineteenth-century practice, among the upper classes, of taking a journey after the wedding became assimilated to the honeymoon concept, and soon the two were indistinguishable.

CARRYING THE BRIDE OVER THE THRESHOLD

This custom, which comes from the ancient Mediterranean, is a curious piece of mock chivalry that reflects the human male's concern about female power. Many commentators have seen the practice as a survival of marriage by capture: The groom was forced to carry his captive bride over the doorstep because that was the only way she would go. The chivalrous interpretation, which sees the husband helping his beloved over a tricky obstacle, is a subtle variation of this capture scenario. In both tableaux, the impotence of the bride is emphasized, while the husband is depicted as being in charge. But these readings of the custom are misleading.

Originally, brides were lifted over thresholds not because they were too weak to negotiate the boundary, but because they were too strong. A new bride was an extremely powerful figure, indeed a dangerous one, and precautions had to be taken lest she bring bad luck into the house. It was especially important to take these precautions at the entrance to the dwelling, for doorways were likewise powerful places. Potentially threatening spirits lived at thresholds, and it was always wise to propitiate them before entering; this is the likely origin, for example, of the protective *mezzuzah* on Jewish doorframes. The bride was lifted over the doorsill because, as a stranger, she was taboo. It was only after she had actually entered the room—after she had, in effect, been sneaked past the guard—that the contagion of taboo was considered lifted. The entire scenario is a vivid survival of passage rites, which, as Arnold Van Gennep made clear, were created to circumvent the dangers involved with "threshold states."

ANNIVERSARY GIFTS

The conservative Emily Post observes that until "comparatively modern times," only eight anniversaries were designated as requiring traditional gifts:

the first: paper
the fifth: wood
the tenth: tin
the fifteenth: crystal
the twentieth: china
the twenty-fifth: silver
the fiftieth: gold
the sixtieth: diamond

However, the convention of assigning traditional presents to other anniversaries was well-established by the middle of the nineteenth century. E. Cobham Brewer, writing in 1870, recorded designated gifts for the first fifteen anniversaries, for the decades and half-decades from twenty to sixty, and for seventy-five, which, like sixty, required diamonds.

The logic of Brewer's and other traditional listings is that of hierarchical value, based on market prices. The anniversary gift catalog thus provides one of those rare cases—so comforting to lovers of consistency—in which the symbolic and economic interpretations of a custom reinforce rather than undermine each other. One celebrates the first year of marriage with paper, which is easily obtainable, and escalates to items of increasing material worth with each new year of bliss attained. The idea is that happiness, or at least stability, deserves rewards, and the more stability the greater the reward. In a sense, therefore, the list is a bribe, as Post was quick to imply. Reacting harshly against the early-twentieth-century custom of celebrating an "early silver" on the fifth anniversary, she counseled couples not to be impatient. Such an innovation, she said, was "not only incorrect but shocking in its implication of 'We must hurry to celebrate the important weddings while we are still married to each other.' "

EYE OF THE BEHOLDER:

COSTUME AND APPEARANCE

MEN'S TIES

The dangling pieces of fabric that men wear around their necks, at least on important occasions, are derived from a French style that was adopted in the seventeenth century from Croatia. It is uncertain whether the fashion arrived with Croatian immigrants or it was picked up by French soldiers from Croatian soldiers during the Thirty Years' War. In either case the original ties in Western Europe, typically made of white linen, were known as Croatian neckpieces. The source is reflected in our modern, if now somewhat archaic, term *cravat,* from the proper name *Cravate,* for "Croatian."

It is ironic that the tie used to be a sign of a certain exotic raffishness, for today it symbolizes just the opposite. Styles in tie patterns vary from decade to decade, as styles in neckwear have varied considerably since the seventeenth century. But whatever the mode at a given moment, the principle of conformity remains: Nothing quite so succinctly demonstrates the rigidity of commercial dress as the fact that successful men must wear ties, and ties of a particular pattern and hue.

Whatever the fashion mavens dictate, the one thing that is certain is that it will be adopted, and quickly, by every man who aspires to success. The reason for this is that the necktie, far more than any other item of apparel, is an instantly recognizable badge of status. The correct tie indicates not only that you are on your way but that you are sufficiently au courant to understand how to *demonstrate* that you are on your way. That ties are phallic in design corroborates rather than undermines this basic function: The irony of tie-wearing is the psychosexual one that power is demonstrated by conformity.

HIGH HEELS

Why would any woman in her right mind choose to walk on the balls of her feet with her heels propped up by spikes? The historical answer is that high heels reflect aristocratic tastes—specifically, the tastes of the seventeenth-century French court, which first popularized them in Europe. Not only did heels keep the wearer's feet relatively mud free, they also created a physical elevation to match the social elevation of the stylish, exaggerated the strutting gait of the noble classes, and they suggested, by their very precariousness, that their owners could afford not to worry about falling on their faces. Indeed, as Bernard Rudofsky points out, seventeenth-century wearers of high heels, men and women, frequently had to be transported in sedan chairs because they could not manage cobblestones on foot. Some "heels" in that era were actually full-soled platforms, and to walk on these things at all, one needed the constant elbow support of two servants.

The helplessness associated with the raised-heel style encouraged the notion that heeled persons were above having to care for themselves. In view of this, it is not surprising that even today it is women, almost exclusively, who wear heels. High heels are the cobbler's contribution to what I have called the pedestal ploy (see LADIES FIRST). They link physical incapacity with the notion of woman as a "higher being"—too high to get along on her own.

Women have taken to high heels, of course, because they feel, correctly, that they increase their attractiveness to men. Part of that increased attractiveness has to do with male fantasies of female fragility. As fashion iconoclast Elizabeth Hawes puts it, "The idea is that he, in his heavy shoes, should *feel* stronger and more capable than she on her fragile stilts. Never mind the realities." Another part of it may be biological. In his discussion of rump display among mammals, Dale Guthrie notes that the "lines of the buttocks, thigh, calf and ankle have a native sexual stimulation, but this can be increased with high-heeled shoes; the curves are exaggerated when the heel is lifted." Heels also exaggerate the lateral motion of the buttocks. The ultimate function of high heels, therefore, may be to fuel the male belief that women are both impotent and seductive.

DESIGNER CLOTHING

There is nothing novel about people of means advertising their status with expensive, designer-made apparel. What is peculiar is that the owners of the new designer costuming feel obliged to broadcast their taste by displaying labels on the *outside* of their possessions. Judith Martin (1985) relates this development to a growing "tyranny of the commercial classes" and explains that visible labels meet the modern need for the relative worth of purchased goods to be "recognizable to people who haven't had sufficient leisure to learn to make subtle judgments." In the good old days of class rigidities, the owners of Titian paintings or Adolfo gowns needed to impress only their social peers who, like them, *had* had the leisure to learn subtle judgments and who therefore did not need to see the artist's signature in order to be sure of the possession's worth. Today, as more and more of the "uncultured" become millionaires, taste is often confused with the capacity to purchase the latest fad. This crassification of fine judgment is fanned into fever by style merchants. The result, Martin tells us, is that "the rich, who were traditionally courted and served by the commercial classes, have now put themselves at the service of those very persons who have a financial interest in the competition for social standing." Thus "arrival" in the current social sphere means being accepted by one's hairdresser or couturier or headwaiter.

UNIFORMS

The uniforms that are commonly worn today by members of military, religious, professional, and labor organizations bear an important functional relationship to what Erving Goffman (1961) once called the standard-issue "identity kits" of asylums and other "total institutions." The relationship is not accidental. The underlying function of all such regularized garb is the same as that of the prison or asylum inmate's standard fare: to suppress the individuality of the wearer and thus to forge a conceptual union between the goals of the institutional member and the goals of the institution itself. By definition, no uniform can make an individual statement. A uniform identifies its wearer as a team player who will not make waves, who agrees to subordinate personal tastes and interests to the good of the whole. In this sense the soldier, the pin-striped executive, and the football player all share a common mind set.

This is seldom a problem for the soldier, because individuality of thought in the military is a contradiction in terms; the entire point of military discipline is to follow orders so that the team can win. (Frederick II put a fine point on this observation when he said that if any of his own troops started to think, he would lose his army overnight.) Uniformity of dress becomes an issue only when those being dressed in standard issue are unwilling to kneejerk to institutional designs. Hence the ongoing battle in hospital nursing against "starch and caps" dress codes. As the more independent-minded nurses point out, the requirement of uniforms for nurses, far from enhancing their professional image, actually reinforces their subordination. If standard dress were a sign of higher rather than lower status, the physicians would wear the caps.

BLUE JEANS

Blue jeans are so widely recognized as typically American that the nation's chief storehouse of Americana, the Smithsonian Institution, keeps several pairs in its permanent collection. Their creator was a young dry-goods peddler named Levi Strauss, who had followed the Forty-Niners to California in 1850, intending to sell them tent canvas. When he discovered that they needed sturdy pants much more than tents, he began turning the canvas into "waist overalls" and soon set up shop in San Francisco.

His business took off, and a lesser man might have been content, but Levi had his sights on perfection. In the next decade he introduced three design changes that were to make the name *levis* synonymous the world over with "blue jeans." One was the addition of the reinforcing rivets that have remained his company's trademark. Another was the substitution for canvas of a durable cotton called *serge de Nimes,* named for its French town of origin. The "de Nimes" cloth soon became "denim." The third was the use of an indigo dye that he found he could depend on for consistent color; and thus the "blue" jean was born.

FALL SHOPPING SPREES

The obvious reason that fall is a season of manic clothes-buying is that students return to school in September, and whether they are six or twenty-six, they want to impress their friends with their new finery. The back-to-school wardrobe has thus become as much a fixture in late-summer advertising as have pleas to stock up on lunchboxes and spiral notebooks.

There may be more than commercial logic to this. For well over 90 percent of our time on this planet, we hominids lived as slowly migrating hunter-gatherers. Throughout our long Stone Age prehistory, and especially during the ice-bound Pleistocene, protection against the savagery of winter depended on an ample supply of warm garments, and signs of approaching winter, such as the falling of leaves, might easily have triggered our brains to step up our attacks on fur-bearing mammals. Although merchandising and peer pressure have done their part to make the fall shopping spree a routine event, it may be that the prototypical objects of September's acquisitiveness were not Izod alligators but the local habitat's wooliest-looking cave bears.

TROUSER CUFFS

Cuffs on sleeves have gone in and out of fashion since the Renaissance, but cuffs on trousers were introduced only about seventy-five years ago. Both these fashion tics probably grew out of the wearer's desire to keep his garments out of something messy. For the wrist cuff, this something was food, and the permanent cuffed sleeve was probably initially a rolled-up sleeve. For the trouser cuff, the offending substance was probably mud. Long pants had come in at the beginning of the nineteenth century, thanks to the fashion innovation of England's Beau Brummel. After a century of slogging around with soiled trouser legs, men finally got the bright idea that rolling them up and out of the mud was a fair tradeoff between comfort and elegance. Shortly before World War I, the improvisation became a fad, and tailors began to sew the cuffs into place.

MALE AND FEMALE BUTTONING

Here's the standard explanation of why men's buttons are on the right side and women's on the left. When buttons were introduced in the Middle Ages, men carried swords under their tunics, and these swords hung on the left side for easier drawing. It was more efficient to place buttons on the right side, so a threatened gentleman could reach for his weapon with his fighting hand while his left hand unbuttoned the garment. Women's buttons were placed on the left because women carried their children on their left hip and therefore preferred to nurse them at the left breast.

This explanation is colorful nonsense. Look at any history of costume. You will see that early (fourteenth-century) buttoning styles could not have been designed for swordsmen. Some tunics had over a dozen buttons down the front; to extract a sword from beneath such a garment while someone was coming at you with a sword would have been a task only a wizard or a fool would have undertaken. Therefore, medieval gentlemen did what anyone would do: They carried their swords *over* their garments, as the picture books clearly show.

As for the second half of the argument, even if it were true that women's garments started out with left-hand buttons (which they didn't in all cases), no woman in her right mind would ever habitually nurse a child on one side; the result would be a lopsided, painful tumidity. In addition, well-born women of the Middle Ages—the ones who could have afforded buttons—would not have been carrying children on either side; their offspring would have been suckled by wetnurses.

Possibly the varying button tradition derives distantly from the ancient symbolism of right and left, which takes the right, or dextrous, side as male and the left, or sinister, side as female. This too is unprovable, and I am inclined, in the absence of any firm evidence, toward a quite mundane explanation. Austin, Texas, newspaper columnist Ellie Rucker once quoted a seamstress on how she remembers which side to put the buttons on. "When you're driving in the car, if the guy is driving, he can see inside your shirt and you can see inside of his." Since Renaissance etiquette insisted that a man always walk on the right, perhaps it was an inversion of this logic, in the direction of modesty, that started the right and left distinction.

LAST BUTTON UNDONE

Both the vest of the modern three-piece suit and the manner of wearing this quite inessential garment are legacies of the British royal line. The vest was introduced in 1666 by King Charles II, who meant it, said Samuel Pepys, "to teach the nobility thrift." (The lesson is obscure; perhaps what the king had in mind was the garment's sleevelessness.) The buttons of this innovation stayed buttoned, from top to bottom, until the beginning of the nineteenth century, when the king-to-be was the Prince of Wales. The prince was an exceptionally portly gadabout who, with his friend Beau Brummel, set many fashions for English polite society. One that was dictated by his girth rather than by any sense of style was the unbuttoning of the final button on vests and jackets alike. It is because the Prince of Wales could not close his bottom button that men of fashion leave theirs open today.

HANDKERCHIEFS

The modern pocket handkerchief, an almost purely decorative item, derives from the more utilitarian hand kerchief of the late Middle Ages and, before that, from the *coverchef* (from the Old French for "head covering") that was introduced into Europe from the East around the thirteenth century. As the name implies, kerchiefs originally functioned as makeshift headwear; only gradually were they dropped to the neck (whence "neckerchief") and then to the hand. During the Renaissance, hand kerchiefs served essentially the same purposes that nineteenth-century cowboy neckerchiefs served in this country. They were useful not only for nose-blowing but also as sweatbands and face mops to remove the dust and grime of a largely outdoor existence. Only recently did this quite utilitarian object move from the hand into the breast pocket. It is a comment, perhaps, on the general squeamishness of our culture regarding dirt that as an accessory, the pocket handkerchief is now decidedly placed "for show, not for blow."

WOMEN'S HEADS COVERED IN CHURCH

In most religions, worshippers uncover their heads before God. Baring the head is a sign of compliance—a sign that you are offering service to one greater than yourself. An exception to this rule is the custom in the Catholic Church of having women keep their heads covered, while men observe the more common rule. The discrepancy is a legacy of St. Paul, who in Chapter 11 of his first letter to the Corinthians distinguished between man as "the image and glory of God" and woman as "the glory of the man." A man should not cover up his glory, but go uncovered (bare-headed), in the sight of the Lord. Merely a reflection of masculine glory, a woman is God's image once removed, so she should have a covering "power on her head" to show she is under the power of her husband (Cor. 11:10). Paul also says that a woman's long hair is "a glory to her," for it is given her as a covering (Cor. 11:15). This seems, inconsistently, to suggest that she too should pray with a bare head. Until the 1960s the Church ignored this inconsistency and required women to cover their heads. This was in accord with what many have felt Paul's underlying message to be: that women should cover up their "glory" because it was a temptation to men.

EARRINGS

Humans wear ornaments on their ears for many of the same reasons that they wear ornaments anywhere else: for status identification and for attracting the opposite (or in some cases, the same) sex. They pierce their ears for the same reason that many Asian and African women put similar holes through their noses. The flesh at those areas of the body may be pierced easily and generally without infection.

But there is another reason for wearing earrings that makes them particularly interesting and that may account, indirectly, for their popularity in our own culture. According to the chroniclers of English superstition E. and M. A. Radford, earrings are often worn as charms: among the general population because they are thought to cure bad eyesight, and among sailors as a protection against drowning. This may explain the traditional popularity of long-loop earrings among pirates.

WRISTWATCHES

Until the end of the nineteenth century, men who were affluent enough to own a watch and educated enough to be able to use one carried their timepieces on fobs or on dangling chains, in their vest pockets. Telling the time in that era involved a brief but impressive social ritual of withdrawing the watch from its compartment, opening the lid, and announcing the time like an alchemist intoning a secret formula. What largely obliterated this ritual was the introduction of the wristwatch—that inexpensive, instantly accessible innovation that, in an age of public education, anybody could read. It was invented in 1907 by French jeweler Louis Cartier, in response to a request by aviator Alberto Santos-Dumont, who wanted to be able to check his flying time in speed trials faster than he could do so with a pocket watch. The invention gained popularity several years later, when French soldiers made use of the easily read wristwatch in the hectic and bloody trenches of World War I. The modern Timex or Rolex, then, distantly recalls that slaughter.

THE SHADES EFFECT

Ostensibly, people wear sunglasses to protect their eyes from excessive light. Although protection is certainly a factor, it is probably not accidental that "shades" have become popular in a century where privacy is increasingly under threat and where the need to look others in the eye, however intimidating that may be, is a daily social demand. For some, sunglasses provide a respite from the visual overload of an intensely gregarious culture. They use them for protection, not from the sun, but from the unwelcome stares of other people. Moreover, with their sun-glasses on, these people are intimidating because they can inspect your eyes—those important registers of emotion—but you cannot inspect theirs. It is because sunglasses effectively, if temporarily, disguise the wearer's weakness that they are most popular among the insecure—that is, among people who cannot show their vul-nerability. The state policeman with his aviator goggles, the pimp with midnight wraparounds, the movie star with her oversized designer Polaroids, all have a turf and a reputation to protect, and none of them can afford to let the casual observer in on the "real" person behind the shades.

EYE SHADOW

The expressive nature of the human eye is largely a function of color contrast, and specifically of the contrast between the white of the sclera and the deeper shades of the iris. In terms of visual attractive-ness, as well as of simple recognition, it is the combination of white-plus-color, not the colored irises alone, that sends out the most commanding signals. Thus you know you are close enough to fire on the enemy when, in Israel Putnam's phrase, you can "see the whites of their eyes." The striking violet of Elizabeth Taylor's eyes would never have merited a line of print were it not set off by the "back-ground" white.

Here lies the seemingly frivolous but actually quite logical reason that women put colored powders and creams on their eyelids. Sur-rounding the eyeball with blue or green adds a second circle of contrast to the existing contrast of iris and sclera, which makes that area attract attention all the quicker.

The rationale (if not the genealogy) of this procedure has been known for centuries. The seventeenth-century writer John Bulwer commented on the Turkish custom of eye-shadowing, which at that time was practiced by both men and women. They paint their eyelids, he said, with a black powder known as *alchole* because it "doth color them black, whereby the white of the Eye is set off more white."

PAINTED LIPS

It's obvious that body decoration is a method of increasing sexual attractiveness and that this is the case whether the decoration is jewelry, tattooing, or cosmetics. But it's not obvious why certain body areas are chosen and why certain decorations are consistently applied to them in certain cultures. The use of red lipstick in many cultures and universally in Western cultures (at least until the advent of the punk phenomenon) is a case in point. Why paint the lips, and why the wide preference for *red?* Two provocative theories are advanced by biologists Desmond Morris and Dale Guthrie.

For Morris, painting the lips red suggests an unconscious impulse to copy the redness of the genital labia of prehominids. In the shift from the typical rear-entry sexuality of baboons and other primates to the frontal position favored by humans, evolution must have devised some signal to make the front of the female body as attractive to the prehistoric male human as the back of the female baboon was to his primate ancestors. In fact, what developed was "frontal self-mimicry," where the fleshy buttocks of the other primates were replicated in the fleshy breasts of the human female, and where the genital labia (which redden naturally during arousal) were replicated by the facial lips. The human preference for face-to-face copulation was reinforced by the female's "duplicate set of buttocks and labia." And further reinforced by lipstick and brassieres.

Guthrie relates red-painted lips to the process of social "neoteny," that is, the adult's retention of juvenile characteristics. Red lips mimic the distended, engorged lips of a suckling baby. Hence "the exaggerated everted lip of the lipstick ad model is similar to the Lifebuoy baby-complexion ad." This interpretation seems to contradict Morris's notion that red lips signal sexual readiness, but only if we assume that such readiness is the prerogative of adults. In a culture which simultaneously infantilizes women and sexualizes children—in which Brooke Shields is a superstar, Barbie dolls sell like hotcakes, and child pornography is big business—the contradiction is more apparent than real.

SUNTANNING

Given the low status that still accompanies naturally dark skin in this country, it seems peculiar that white Americans would conceal their own lightness by tanning. Yet the pasty, spectral look that was favored by the elegant of the last century has now gone completely out of fashion, and it has become quite acceptable—in some circles, even required—to show expanses of well-bronzed skin, especially in the late summer and early fall. The reason for this shift in skin-tone preference probably has to do less with health than with status.

In the last century, wealthy people cultivated a pallid complexion because it distinguished them from the working classes: Scarlett O'Hara's translucent skin indicated that she could afford to stay out of the sun. Today, with far more people working indoors, a light skin no longer signals class in the same way. Inside a massive office building, the mailroom clerk is likely to have the same complexion as the vice-president in charge of marketing. To disguise this unacceptable leveling of visible status, the old relationships between skin tone and class are reversed. The distinguished pallor of the last century becomes the color of closeted, unrelieved labor while the ruddiness of the nineteenth-century farmer becomes the new sign of upward mobility. This is not a capricious association, for only those with sufficient leisure to afford Caribbean vacations or sun rooms are generally able to sport a deep tan. That is why the greatest degree of status to be gained from a tan accrues to the tanee in the winter.

SAILORS' TATTOOS

Tattooing is a common form of body decoration in traditional societies around the world. As R. W. B. Scutt and Christopher Gotch note, the ancient Egyptians almost certainly practiced the art, and there is also some indirect evidence—in the form of needles and "statuettes bearing marks strongly suggestive of tattoos"—that Ice Age humans did too. The social reasons for the practice vary from one place to another. Scutt and Gotch list over a dozen rationales, including such magical reasons as the propitiation of evil spirits and such mundane ones as the indelible registering of medical data, such as the person's blood type. Perhaps the most common reasons for the custom, however, relate to love and war. Certainly among military personnel, the chief fanciers of tattoos in our society, the favored designs have always been metaphors for the battle of the sexes (from bleeding hearts to naked women) or for the supposed sexiness of battle (daggers, death's heads, and coiling dragons).

Tattooing reached the West thanks to Captain Cook, whose sailors copied the idea from South Sea islanders. Like the natives, the English navvies associated the tattooing operation with masculine courage—both the courage it took to endure the setting of the design with needles and the more generalized bravado that was associated with being a member of a fighting elite. There is even some anecdotal evidence that the Western and the Maori attitudes toward tattoo display reflected an identical view of manly status. In eighteenth-century New Zealand, a man unmarked with tattoos was considered a nobody, and tattooing among sailors also came to be seen as a required initiation rite. Getting a tattoo in the military made one an "official" member of the band.

Yet there is another reason for tattooing's popularity among sailors. Men throughout the world may sport daggers to demonstrate their fearlessness and strength (it's not accidental that the arm is usually the site, for the tattoo lends it symbolic potency). But seagoing, womenless men also display nudes and scrolls of sweethearts' names because, like the snapshot in the wallet, these pictures sustain a link to Eros when a more immediate link is not possible. Albert Parry is justified in supposing that for most subjects tattooing is "the recording of dreams."

DEODORANTS

Body odor has always been part of the human experience, but it has been perceived as a social plague only in the past couple of generations, and chiefly by Americans. The largely American custom of abolishing underarm odor has certainly been abetted in this century by the multimillion-dollar cosmetics industry, which simultaneously invented the dire phrase "B.O." and the concoctions to eliminate it. But there may be a broader historical reason for our aversion to our own natural aroma.

Not only are we the descendants of the Puritans, whose suspicion of the body was profound, but we are also the descendants, less distantly, of a potpourri of immigrants, each wave of which had its own cuisine, its own bathing customs, and consequently its own distinct odors. As Margaret Mead pointed out in an interview with Kathrin Perutz, the American deodorizing custom may have grown out of the practical necessity of making different-smelling people less repugnant to each other. Deodorants, therefore, become a kind of olfactory leveling mechanism, obscuring offensive ethnic distinctions and allowing everybody to smell "clean," like America.

Biologist Dale Guthrie says that our nearly unique taboos against scent display have arisen fairly recently and that the enforcement of these taboos may be related to a suppression of territoriality and to a desire to emulate the young. The obvious aim of washing and spraying our armpits may be to make us less offensive (in a physical as well as a social sense) to those with whom we share space, but another, complementary aim is to make us "sweet-smelling like the immature." Perhaps there is a tie-in here with our nation's notorious worship of youth and our fear of growing old and decayed. Disguising our natural scents with deodorants may be a way of disguising our mortality itself.

SHAVING

Long hair on men has been a prime gender signal since early hominid times, and a sign of social status for almost as long. It is puzzling, therefore, that so many men, in so many different cultures, should choose to shave off their beards—to adopt, in effect, the appearance of a slave or a child. Dale Guthrie relates this curious custom to a desire to appear less threatening to others: "A shaven male runs himself back down the hierarchy spectrum so that he can enjoy to some extent the protections given pre-puberty males." This strategem, Guthrie suggests, is appropriate in a complex society such as ours, where "a social posture of cooperation" may be more effective than brute force.

Although this is an interesting analysis, things were complicated early on when military units adopted shaving as a form of uniform discipline. Legend says that Alexander the Great demanded that his troops be clean-shaven so the enemy could not grab them by their beards. The picture was further complicated by the swings of fashion occasioned by rulers' ability or inability to grow beards. And once alternative fashions were established, Desmond Morris (1985) notes, "it became possible for any social group or culture to make a statement of allegiance or rebellion by the way their males trimmed their beards." Thus beards became once again symbols of status, only now of varying and vying kinds of status.

The equation of hairlessness with powerlessness works better when the shaver is a woman. It is certainly not without significance that females have been removing their body hair longer than males. The modern depilatory business only capitalizes on a longstanding tradition of women plucking their eyebrows, shaving the hair off their legs, having their pubic hair removed by airbrush in the centerfolds of girlie magazines, and even removing the tufts of hair in their armpits which, biologically speaking, act as a sexually stimulating "scent trap." The overall effect of such depilation, if Morris and Guthrie are right, is to make the female symbolically as nonthreatening as the nakedest of the naked apes—the human infant. It was in reaction to this implied infantilization, of course, that feminists in the 1970s experimented with hirsute femininity.

TABLE MATTERS:

FOODWAYS

COOKING FOOD

Peter Farb and George Armelagos tell us that the human preference for cooked food "must have developed gradually over a very long period of time as the advantages came to be recognized." These advantages would have included the destruction of bacteria and toxins and the greater digestibility of heated food. Cooking amounts to "a sort of external predigestion." So far, so good, but the question remains: Why think of cooking in the first place?

This is one of those fascinating questions (like, who invented the wheel?) where the best answer is still happy accident. The English essayist Charles Lamb, in his amusing "Dissertation on Roast Pig," suggested that cooking was invented after a Chinese boy, poking about in the ashes of a burned hut, tasted a pig that had died there. Others have set this prehistoric tableau in a burned forest and mused that hot meat might have tasted good because it reminded those early humans of the freshly killed prey of prehominid days. This argument, of course, assumes collective memory and a carnivorous ancestry, both of which scientists are still debating.

Dismissing such whimsies, Farb and Armelagos suggest that religion was involved. Many ancient rituals called for the burning of sacrificial animals so that the aromatic smoke would reach the gods. Such sacrifices were later consumed, and in this way humans may have developed a taste for roasted meat. A taste for cooked plant food may have followed as a matter of extrapolation and experiment, or it too may have come about by accident. It is not hard to imagine the first baked potato as one that was dropped in the hearth by a clumsy genius. Once our ancestors discovered that cooked plants were easier to chew, haute cuisine was just around the corner.

THREE MEALS A DAY

Although two was the official number of meals in the Middle Ages—thanks to ecclesiastical insistence on fasting—this official pattern was frequently modified on pragmatic grounds. Laborers, the sick, the very young, and the very old were permitted a third meal in the morning (a breaking of the fast, or "breakfast") for health reasons. This modification caught on, and by the seventeenth century three meals a day, Michael Carroll points out, "had become *both* the norm *and* the practice at all levels of society." It remains the publicly acknowledged norm even today, and there may be a bioenergetic logic to this. After running computerized tests of the body's energy needs, psychologist David Booth concluded that this pattern may be "well-adapted motivationally and nutritionally to the average physiology of an adult with a sedentary lifestyle."

I say "publicly acknowledged" norm, however, because, in fact, the three-meal-a-day pattern is not the total reality today. We *speak* about eating three meals a day, quite possibly, for the same reason that we speak reverently of the Trinity, or that we acknowledge the triangle as a geometric "good figure"—because the number 3 has had a mystical, comforting significance for Western minds since the days of Pythagoras. In fact, considering the prevalence of snacking in our culture, it would be more correct to say that the norm is six or seven "meals" a day.

WHY DO WE USE FORKS?

Since the vast majority of the world's population continues to do without forks—preferring chopsticks or those old standbys, the fingers—it is quite reasonable to ask why we in the West have so long found them essential. Three related answers suggest themselves.

First, our diet, unlike that of the rest of the world, is extremely meat-heavy, and while it is certainly possible to eat a chunk of beef with the fingers, the grease and potential burn factors are considera-

bly higher here than they are in picking up boiled rice. Forks may
have become popular here to offset these culinary hazards or to allow
greedy diners to skewer the largest bites more efficiently.

Second, Westerners are less communal (in the sense of being less
comfortable with close contact) than the rest of the world. The
individual fork may enjoy its vogue here because it heightens social
distance. Indeed, individual place settings, and individual dining
forks, arose in the fifteenth century, at precisely the time that greater
social mobility and interclass contact were making common-pot dining—until then the norm—seem especially unattractive.

Last, but certainly not least, we can understand the fork—and its
spinoffs the dessert fork, the salad fork, and the oyster fork—as part
of that efflorescence of the inutile that always accompanies the rise
of new money. Renaissance fatcats may have started the tradition,
but the true flowering of table utensils came a few centuries later,
during America's Gilded Age. Arthur Schlesinger identifies "the cult
of the fork" as part of that age's noted propensity for artifice and
conspicuous display.

ZIGZAG EATING

In Europe you hold the fork in your left hand and the knife in your
right throughout the meal—a system that everyone agrees is more
efficient than our zigzag method. No authorities find the American
style "incorrect," although they all concur it is eccentric. Where and
why it arose they do not say. A few suggestions:

(1) Americans are practical and efficient. Since most of us are
right-handed, it makes sense to keep our working tools at all times
in the hand that can wield them most effectively.

(2) Americans are rebels. We adopted the zigzag method to break
the rules, as a way of thumbing our noses at Mother England.

(3) Americans are a restless breed. We do not like to sit in one spot
for very long, and when dining forces us to do so, we respond by
juggling the silver.

Whatever the reason for the practice, it is now certainly as American as apple pie. Europeans gleefully recognize this and are quick to
pounce on it as evidence of our innocence of form. My father, in Paris
during the last war, discovered this to his humiliation. Lunching at

a sidewalk cafe one day with a beret on his head, a Gauloise in the ashtray, and a copy of *Le Monde* on the table, he looked every centimeter a Frenchman. As he was dissecting his food, however, a real Frenchman sat down nearby and inquired politely and without a moment's hesitation, "Do you have the time, sir?" He had been betrayed by his zigzag hands.

Arguments against the zigzag method rest not only on grounds of efficiency but also on those of tradition. In Old World dining, the knife was held in the right hand continually because it could serve as an instant defense should your soiree suddenly be crashed by an uninvited Saracen, Visigoth, or neighbor. Such vigilance is out of place on these shores not only because of the shortage of Saracens but also because, as any good patriot will tell you, this is the home of the brave. We juggle our silverware, perhaps, to show that we are not afraid—that one of us holding a fork is worth any number of them holding blades.

ELBOWS OFF THE TABLE

Most table manners, now as in the late Middle Ages when the idea of table manners was born, have a fairly obvious utilitarian function. They keep one from offending fellow diners by the intrusion on their territory or by the desecration of common ground. Thus one does not wave a fork or a knife in another's direction, reach across another's chest for the potatoes, or sneeze into the centerpiece. The overall goal, as Norbert Elias observed about manners in general, is to maintain social distance between the classes and, as those classes inevitably mix in modern society, to maintain a semblance of integral privacy among members of the same social class.

The old chestnut about keeping your elbows off the table is related, albeit obliquely, to this basic distancing rule. Elbows are banned because an elbow on the table encroaches on common, interdiner space. It is a subtly aggressive social action, hinting that expansion may be in the offing and that your dinner partner had better watch his borders. While admitting that the fugitive single elbow near the plate is "no longer punishable by hanging," Miss Manners (Martin, 1982) says it is still "a good rule to keep one's arms close to the body." Why? So that they stay out of your neighbor's ribs.

SAYING GRACE

In the religious sense, grace is a gift of God, that divine, merciful generosity that can be neither earned nor deserved. To fundamentalist Christians, it is the only thing that can get you saved. In the mundane sense, grace, whether physical or social, is something you're born with, something you either have or you don't. So it seems odd to "say" a grace actively—and even odder in older parlance, when you "made," "gave," or "rendered" a grace—for how can you give something over which you have no control?

The answer to this confusion can be found in Rome, because it is from the Latin *gratia* that we get the English word *grace.* The root meaning of *gratia* was "that which is pleasing or agreeable," and the Romans were the first to expand this meaning into the two nuances I have just mentioned. They took *gratia* as "favor" or "kindness" (which led to the religious sense of unearned gift) and as "popularity" or "esteem" (which led to grace in the sense of human charm). But they also took it to mean one more thing: the thanks that an agreeable or pleasing person would be likely to give *and* to receive. It is from this third sense of *gratia* that our grace at meals ultimately derives. It is the grace we return to the Almighty for the grace He has given, or may give, us. Spanish, of course, retains this third nuance in everyday speech: the most mundane favor merits a *"gracias."*

BACON AND EGGS

Eggs and some form of pork—usually bacon, but often sausage or ham—constitute the traditional American breakfast. This grease-lover's special reflects the earliest colonists' affection for the pig. Not until the mid-nineteenth-century push toward manifest destiny had brought white settlers to the prairies did beef become king in the states. Up to that time, the pig, which required less care than cattle, because it could forage for itself in the thicketed woodlands of the East, was the domestic meat of choice. The seventeenth-century American expression "high on the hog" refers to the association of wealth with an abundance of pork. Marvin Harris (1985) quotes a facetious Georgia doctor from the early 1800s who advocated renaming the United States either the "Republic of Porkdom" or the "Great Hog-Eating Confederacy." And, in spite of the introduction of steak and eggs onto restaurant menus, our 300-year-old mania for eating pork with our eggs lives on today.

Why eggs? Waverley Root and Richard de Rochemont suggest that pigs and chickens took hold in the early colonies because they were the easiest animals to transport by ship from the Old World and because they could provide supplemental food on an unexpectedly long voyage. Eggs probably became popular specifically at breakfast because they are freshest when just gathered from the previous night's roosting.

CORNFLAKES FOR BREAKFAST

Before around 1900, the idea of eating cornflakes for breakfast would not have occurred to the average American, for the simple reason that dry cereal had not been invented yet. The person responsible for this relatively young American tradition was a vegetarian health faddist named John Harvey Kellogg. In the 1890s Kellogg, a physician and a Seventh-Day Adventist, was medical superintendent of the Battle Creek Sanitarium, a Michigan clinic that had been founded by his sect in 1860 as the Western Health Reform Institute. For his sickly, carnivorous clientele, Kellogg devised a meatless, low-dairy regimen which he called the "Battle Creek Idea." Included in it were a battery of dried and flaked cereals and what we today call granola.

These innovations would have profited only Kellogg's own patients had it not been for two other men. One was Kellogg's brother Will, who founded what is now the largest cereal company in the world. The other was a salesman named Charles William Post, a Seventh-Day Adventist with his eye on more than spiritual matters. As a patient of Kellogg's in 1891, Post saw the market possibilities of grains, set up his own spa and business, and was soon rivaling his mentor with such products as Postum, Grape-Nuts, and Post Toasties.

Eccentricity attended the two cereal giants throughout their lives. J. H. Kellogg, creator of the best-selling breakfast cereal ever (Kellogg's Corn Flakes), spoke and wrote tirelessly against such evils of

civilization as alcohol, tobacco, and masturbation. Post became a
Texas rancher, experimented with rainmaking, and was the most
virulent anti-unionist of his day. Perhaps the greatest oddity is
the commercial legacy of these two health-food zealots: The companies that grew out of their work are now marketing such "natural"
breakfast delights as Super Sugar Crisp, Frosted Rice, and Froot
Loops.

THE BUSINESS LUNCH

For about the past two decades, the expressions "Let's have lunch"
and (in Hollywood) "Let's do lunch" really have meant "Let's eat
and drink too much while we negotiate a multimillion-dollar deal."
The vogue of the so-called power lunch coincides nicely with the
rambunctious, merger-mad 1970s, when billions of dollars of paper
assets were traded around three-martini tables, and where all the
wheeling and dealing went, conveniently, on the tax tab of John Q.
Public. The "writeoff-ability" of the business lunch, indeed, was one
reason for its immense appeal. Another reason was probably the
opportunity it gave rising executives to engage in the conspicuous
consumption and conspicuous display that are so essential to forging
an upwardly mobile identity. The macho competitiveness underlying
the power lunch was demonstrated by the fact that the "winner" in
such engagements was the person who, after the three martinis, was
still forceful enough to reach for the check.
    Thus the power lunch system was built on two peculiarities of the
American business system: the importance of clout (as opposed to
seat-of-the-pants labor) and the presence of a favorable tax code. At
the beginning of the 1980s, with both these prerequisites going by the
boards, the power lunch was on its way out. Eric Gelman points
clearly to the reasons in his prophetic article "Let's Not Have
Lunch": Corporate honchos in the 1980s are suffering ever-increas-
ing workloads in a highly competitive and highly volatile atmosphere
where you can't write off all you used to. Even if you manage to stay
clearheaded throughout a two-hour lunch, stock markets today
move so rapidly that you are likely to find, when you saunter back
to the office at 3 P.M., that you have missed a major swing. For this
reason, many more male executives are following the lead of up-

wardly mobile women, by eating lunch at their desks to demonstrate that they are constantly on the job.

SALAD BEFORE THE ENTREE

Until about the middle of the nineteenth century, Americans didn't have to worry about whether the salad came before or after the main course, since they didn't eat salads at all. Staunchly carnivorous, they preferred to get their greens indirectly, after they had been processed by rabbits or deer. What shifted public taste toward the salad was the ingenuity of New York's Delmonico brothers, who made their famous nineteenth-century restaurant a smorgasbord of European oddities. By the end of the century, with such novelties as the Waldorf salad sweeping the country, it was no longer considered sissified to chomp on greens.

Europeans still chomp on them *after* the main course, as a way of clearing the palate and of readying the body for the cheese. Why Americans eat their salad first is uncertain. Judith Martin (1982) suggests, with tongue well in cheek, that the custom may be related to the slimming craze ("Fill up on salad first"); to the orneriness of Californians, whose lettucomania is matched only by their frenzy "to do everything differently from normal people"; or to restaurants' desire to keep people busy while the main courses are being prepared. These are sensible, if facetious, suggestions, to which I will add one of my own. In a nation where activity in itself is seen as virtuous, eating raw food while one waits for the cooked food may be a way of announcing that one is not wasting time. Restaurants would naturally encourage this pre–main course exercise because rabbit food is so much cheaper than rabbit: The meagerness of a meal is less noticeable if it comes with a "free" salad bar.

TV DINNERS

In the much-reported breakdown of the American family in this century, one little-noticed cause may have been the introduction of the TV dinner. Norge Jerome notes that the C. A. Swanson Company came out with the first models in 1953, and that they were immediately hailed as a major advance in "convenience." Along with convenience, though, came fragmentation. These lap-tray miracles helped to undermine the principal binding ritual of family life, the communal evening meal.

Before the advent of television, the typical American supper was a community affair in three stages. In the preparation stage, the children frequently helped with table setting while Mother put the last touches on the roast. In the eating stage, more than food was consumed, as family members talked about the day's activities and thus reinforced the group's solidarity. The children again were involved in the cleaning-up stage, so that, as in the first two stages, their significance to the home community was clear. Television attacked only the eating stage, by making it possible to watch and eat simultaneously, effectively killing conversation. It was a combination of thirty-minute programming, the lap tray, and TV dinners that did in the preparation and the cleanup stages. These were eased out by a product that could go from oven to lap, and from lap to garbage pail, with nothing more required of the diners than the use of a fork.

By the beginning of the 1980s, the typical American family dinner was just twenty minutes long. The rapidity of this once-leisurely experience is clearly connected to the overall pace of modern life, but a model for it may have been provided by TV dinners—meals designed to be consumed between the opening and closing credits of a half-hour program.

THE ALL-AMERICAN HAMBURGER

This "traditional" American dish is neither very American nor very traditional. As its name indicates, it probably originated in northern Germany, although some food experts suggest that the first-ever "hamburger" meat was steak tartare—that raw-beef delicacy from, of all places, Mother Russia. Wherever it came from, ground beef as a main course was served only occasionally in nineteenth-century American restaurants, and always without the roll and the "fixin's."

John Mariani tells us that the first hamburger on a roll appeared in this country only a little before World War I: the innovation only really took off with the success of the White Castle chain in the 1920s. As "hamburger stands" modeled on the White Castles began to line American roads, the concept of ground beef on a bun spread because Americans were on the move, touring and looking for employment in the 1930s. Similarly, the proliferation of McDonald's hamburgers in the 1950s was related to the Interstate Highway System and to postwar mobility and suburbanization.

Indeed, as Eric Ross has shown, the American taste for cow meat itself is a relatively recent development, also tied to technological changes. Before the westward expansion of the 1870s, Americans were a nation of pork-eaters. This was appropriate for a population concentrated in the wooded East, since swine take to this kind of terrain. Our appetite for beef was created by the expansion of the railroads into the pasture-rich (and thus cow-appropriate) West, the invention of refrigerator cars that could transport Western beef to Eastern markets, and a rising demand for a beef "byproduct," cowhide, by an expanding leather industry.

WHY IS MCDONALD'S SO SUCCESSFUL?

Archaeologists unearthing the remains of past civilizations frequently come across artifacts that they cannot explain but that, because they are so commonly found, are assumed to have had an intense social or religious meaning to their owners. A thirtieth-century archaeologist digging up our remains would never guess that our soaring "golden arches" had a merely gastronomic significance. Surely our excavator would conclude that they marked the locations of temples or shrines.

In fact, Conrad Kottak (1978) says that eating at McDonald's is "comparable in some respects to a religious ritual." Religious rituals are characterized by "stylized, repetitive, and stereotyped" behaviors that "translate enduring messages, values, and sentiments into observable action." This all fits pretty well, and if the stylized delivery of down-home values is not enough to convince you of the ritualistic character of the McDonald's experience, Kottak asks you to consider the formalized dress of the servers, the incantatory nature of their speech, and the nearly liturgical cast of the menu. To this we might add founder Ray Kroc's obsession with cleanliness and hominess, which hint at the spiritual affinity among God, country, and a double fries.

THE BACKYARD BARBECUE

Folks still eat charcoal burgers in the backyard, but they don't necessarily come off the family grill. In a world where Burger King can deliver a charbroiled patty "your way" in thirteen and a half seconds, there's less point than there used to be in doing it yourself. A major incentive for the rise of backyard grilling in the 1950s was Mom's desire to get out of the kitchen. Today she can do that at a fast-food chain and be freed of the cleanup too. So it may not be going too far to say that the decline in backyard barbecues in this generation has been hastened by automotive mobility.

Ironically it was that very mobility that gave birth to the custom in the first place. Suburban grilling, like suburbia itself, represented a symbolic recapturing of a preindustrial life style. It appeared in the decade when the sourer fruits of industrialism—crowded cities and the ubiquitous automobile—were transforming the country into a mosaic of metrogrids. People moved to the suburbs for more "space," to be sure, but one of the promises of that space was the spaciousness of pre-urban mentalities: the consciousness that there was still "free" land for the taking, where a man could grow (or kill) his own food, far from the clatter of subways. This consciousness, of course, was a lie, since suburbia was the child of the city and so were its barbecue-pit heavens. The put-it-together-yourself "campfires" of the 1950s, contained comfortably within hurricane fences, were the perfect expression of what a critic of mass culture once called America's genius for "packaging marginality." As vividly as the Davy Crockett caps of the same period, they represented the commidification of nostalgia.

OF MEN AND MEAT

In hunting-and-gathering societies, labor is divided strictly by gender. Men hunt. Women, impeded from hunting as they nurse children, gather roots, nuts, and berries. This basic division is retained even today. Women do the "gathering" at the supermarket and retain sovereignty over most of the cooking, but men preserve an exceptional relationship to meat.

It is Dad who turns the steak in the barbecue pit and sometimes even in the kitchen broiler, both of which customs are throwbacks to the hunter's control over game. The ancient hunter returning with a haunch of wild boar not only had physical possession of the meat; no doubt he had tasted some in the wild, raw or cooked over a trail fire. Hence the fondness of "real men" for rare or raw meat and the connection of modern fathers to the outdoor grill. Dad supervises the grilling of the meat because he is captain of carnivores, because he must show he does not fear the flames, and because he knows how to build a fire (a skill whose demonstration has been seriously impaired by the introduction of charcoal and lighter fluid).

It is also Dad who does the carving. No matter how much time Mom has spent basting the oven roast, it is still Dad who handles the blade. Peter Farb and George Armelagos observe that the indoor roast is "ritually butchered at the dinner table by the senior male in the household, wielding a weapon larger than a carving knife need be"; that is, a weapon closer to a small sword than to a slicing instrument. Again there is an unstated recognition of the male's fearlessness. Carving knives are kept razor-sharp and out of reach of the children for more than practical reasons. By keeping such items "out of harm's way," we acknowledge their danger—danger that can only be managed by their "owner." Thus the carving ritual, like the meat-turning ritual, celebrates the male's role as "hunter" while obscuring the equally essential contribution of female "gatherers."

KETCHUP

In defining a national cuisine, Elisabeth Rozin suggests that the meats or vegetables consumed as actual dishes may be less important than the seasonings. Flavoring, she says, provides a "taste marker" for individuals familiar with the cuisine, and that marker defines the cuisine whatever the body of the meal.

If Americans have such a flavor marker, it surely must be ketchup. There is a certain nationalistic justice in this, for the tangy blend that we know as ketchup today was introduced in the centennial year of

1876 by pickle king Henry J. Heinz. At that time "ketchups" had been used for generations by the Chinese (the term is from the Chinese *ke tsiap,* for pickled fish), and they had been known in the Americas for a century, brought there by Yankee sailors. Until the 1870s, people made ketchups at home, by marinating ingredients as diverse as walnuts and blueberries and cucumbers. It wasn't until they discovered, in the 1820s, that the notoriously "poisonous" tomato was good to eat that the groundwork was laid for Heinz's coup. Heinz's formula owed its distinctiveness not only to tomatoes but also to another New World culinary innovation, sugar. Capitalizing on the public's growing sweet tooth, Heinz made a killing literally by sweetening the pot.

HOT DOGS AT BALL GAMES

German-speaking Europe mastered sausage-making during the late Middle Ages, and it was in this meat-loving region that the hot dog was born. Its creator, a German butcher named Johann Georg Lahner (1772–1845), developed prototypes first in Frankfurt and later in Vienna (hence "frankfurter" and "wiener"). Lahner's franks, along with many other types of sausage, were brought to America by German immigrants in the middle of the nineteenth
century.

According to the Oscar Mayer Company, the nation's leading hot dog manufacturer, both the name and the association with baseball games came about simultaneously on a cold April day in 1900. The place was New York City's Polo Grounds, home of the New York Giants. Concessionaire Harry Stevens, having no luck selling ice cream and soda, sent out for Lahner-style franks. Advertising them as "dachshund sausages," he sold them "red hot" to the fans, one of whom was cartoonist Tad Dorgan. Dorgan sketched a dachshund in a roll, and the American hot dog was born.

An alternative tale has the hot-dog-on-a-bun introduced at the 1904 St. Louis World's Fair by German concessionaire Anton Feuchtwanger. To permit his customers to handle the hot sausages without burning their fingers, he lent them gloves when he sold them the dog. When few of the loaned gloves came back, Feuchtwanger switched to the idea of a roll. Luckily, his brother-in-law was a baker, and together they invented the hot dog bun.

SUBMARINE SANDWICH

Whether you call it a submarine sandwich, a hoagie, a grinder, a poor boy, a rocket, a torpedo, an Italian sandwich, or a hero, this concoction of cold cuts on a roll is as quintessentially American as the hot dog or the deep-dish apple pie. In attempting to track down its origin, Edwin Eames and Howard Robboy found that several U.S. cities claim to be its birthplace—the likeliest candidates are New Orleans, New York, Philadelphia, and Chester, Pennsylvania—and concluded that simultaneous, independent invention was a strong possibility. Wherever it started, the sub was clearly an innovation that grew out of the immigrant Italian milieu. Eames and Robboy see it as a compromise between the Old World attachment to sausages and cheeses and the need, in the American workaday context, for an inexpensive yet filling meal that could be carried, without damage, to the workplace. Italian workers in the old country had gone home at midday for their dinner; since U.S. factory owners frowned on this practice, employees adopted the roll as a kind of impromptu lunchbox, and carried their meat and cheese with them.

The sub remained largely a working-class item from its beginning in the 1880s until the Depression, when the financially strapped middle class realized its value as an economy meal and transformed it into an American staple. Eames and Robboy call this an example of the "trickle up" process.

FISH ON FRIDAY

The fish-and-chips and clam chowder specials that so many restaurants offer on Fridays are a secular survival of religious customs that go back to the beginning of Christianity. Jesus and the Apostles, like their fellow Jews and like the shamans of traditional societies, recognized that going without food was a means not only of "mortifying" the body but of intensifying spiritual insight. They recommended fasting to accompany prayer, and the Church fathers followed their lead. Throughout most of Christian history, although local customs have differed, the faithful have been enjoined to practice both fasting and abstinence during Lent and on various Church holidays. By *fasting,* the Church means taking only one meal a day, generally after mid-afternoon; by *abstinence* it means the avoidance of certain foods. The foods prohibited by the custom of abstinence have varied from time to time, but generally animal flesh has been forbidden and often dairy products and eggs as well. From about the ninth century onward, fish was exempted from the "no meat" stricture, and for that reason it became a common food for abstainers. It was especially evident on Fridays because Fridays were designated days of abstinence in commemoration of the Friday Crucifixion. Since the days of Vatican II, the Church has deemphasized fasting and abstinence, since it had become clear by that time that a lobster dinner, or an all-you-can-eat fried clam special at Howard Johnson's, tends to distract the faithful from the spiritual aspects of denial that the custom is supposed to enhance.

WHITE BREAD

Wherever you stand on the nutritional value of white bread, it would be difficult to imagine a better symbol of the homogeneity and predictability of American society. Even though Wonder Bread has responded to consumer pressure and is now producing a whole-wheat alternative, to most of the world we are still a white bread society.

In terms of our advertising and marketing of the bread, it's a fair rap, but in terms of historical development, the chief blame goes to the Hungarians. It was in wheat-rich Hungary in the 1840s that millers first started using roller mills instead of the time-honored but less efficient rotary millstones. And it was from Hungary that roller milling spread throughout Europe and America in the ensuing three decades. Roller milling had two advantages for the miller: It was quicker than stone grinding, and it removed the bran and germ of the wheat, which had contributed to early spoilage and short shelf

life. The down side was that the germless, branless bread was devital-
ized. Bakers got over this minor hurdle by convincing buyers that
white bread was superior.

To be fair to the nineteenth-century baking industry, the rapid
adoption of white bread resulted not so much from a merchant's plot
as from the public's liking for whiteness. White bread made from
stone-ground flour had been the fare of the European nobility for
centuries, and as H.D. Renner argues fairly convincingly, housewives had long been fond of white flour because it rises more predictably and quickly than whole-wheat flour. Add to this the West's
traditional association of white with purity, and it becomes clear that
the white bread society was really the product of developing technology, public ignorance, and symbolic bias.

POTATO CHIPS

The potato chip's original moniker was "Saratoga potato" or
"Saratoga chip," after its birthplace, the fashionable nineteenth-
century resort town of Saratoga Springs, New York. The Saratoga
Chamber of Commerce offers two versions of its origin. Both versions are set in Cary B. Moon's Lake House Restaurant, a favorite
watering hole of railroad baron William K. Vanderbilt. According
to the first version, assistant cook "Aunt Katie" Weeks was frying
crullers one day in 1853, when she accidentally dropped a potato
peeling into the fat, fished it out, and was astounded when chief cook
George Crum, nonchalantly chomping on the morsel, told her it was
delicious. In the second version, Crum himself was responsible, and
the motive was not accident but pique. An overly fastidious diner
sent some french fries back to Crum's kitchen, complaining that they
were not crisp enough. To fix the customer's wagon, the notoriously
cantankerous Crum sliced some potatoes paper thin, chilled them in
ice water to stiffen them, and fried them to the brittleness of dry
twigs. To Crum's chagrin, the fussy diner wolfed them down and
asked for more. Within months they were appearing as freebies on
every bar and tabletop in Saratoga, and by the turn of the century
they had become an American institution, which gradually spread
worldwide.

POPCORN AT THE MOVIES

Like maple syrup and the tomato, popcorn was a gift from the New World to the Old. Radiocarbon testing has dated ears of New Mexican popping corn at 5,600 years old, and paleobotanists now generally agree that popcorn was the earliest form of maize. Columbus in the West Indies and Cortes in Mexico both found the native populations utilizing popped corn as decorations, prefiguring today's popcorn "necklaces." Indians on both continents knew popcorn as food, and they used an ingenious variety of popping methods. Some tribes used hot stones as popping griddles, others threw the unpopped kernels in the fire directly, and others roasted entire ears on stick spits. The pre-Incan populations of Peru even fashioned popcorn poppers out of clay.

The popping custom caught on slowly with Europeans, however, and it wasn't until the early twentieth century that popcorn became a universal American snack. This was due largely to Cloid H. Smith, an Iowa farm boy who formed the American Pop Corn Company in 1914 and began selling his Jolly Time brand shortly after. Gradually, home popping became a national fad.

The introduction of popcorn into movie theaters did not happen until a decade and a half later. According to Moskowitz and his colleagues, theater managers in the 1920s usually barred popcorn from the premises, because their patrons were distracted by the crunching. They relented only in the 1930s, after having been hounded for years by vendors selling under their marquees. Moskowitz and his colleagues suggest that the managers changed their minds because they needed cash during the Depression and sought it from lobby concessions. This is not as plausible as it seems, for the movie industry actually thrived in those years, as the American public's need for escapist entertainment helped to fuel Hollywood's Golden Age. A more likely explanation is that with the introduction of sound in the late 1920s, theatergoers were no longer distracted by the crunching and could use popcorn as they had long used chewing gum—as a means of registering, and defusing, dramatic tension.

"AS AMERICAN AS APPLE PIE"

Although the apple did not originate in America, the expression "as American as apple pie" is, as historian Peter Wynne points out, "not the product of an overzealous imagination," for in colonial times the apple was a mainstay of both plain and fancy cooking. English colonists had brought a taste for the fruit with them from the Old World and began planting orchards as early as 1625. The first Massachusetts governor, William Endicott, was one of many avid planters who helped to lay the groundwork for an industry that today produces over 180 million bushels of the fruit a year.

A major attraction of the apple for the colonists, Wynne says, was that it could be converted into cider. Among people who harbored the common European suspicion of drinking water, and whose grape-growing was inhibited by plant lice, cider became an alternative to wine. Cheap and easy to produce, it was the American drink of choice well into the nineteenth century.

Dried, raw, and cooked, the apple also found its way into numerous colonial dishes, including applesauces, puddings, stuffings, and many desserts. John Mariani is doubtless right in suggesting that apple pie became known as "American," not because it was invented here (in fact, Europeans had been eating apple pies for centuries), but because, thanks to the enormous orchards of Washington and New York states, the United States became the world's largest apple-producing nation.

ICE CREAM CONES

Waverley Root and Richard de Rochemont note that ice cream is so thoroughly "a symbol of America" that during World War II "it was discouraged in Japan as indicating a suspicious sympathy with the enemy." If the anecdote is true, it indicates a misplaced reaction, for the originators of ice cream, at least in the West, were Japan's Axis comrades the Italians. The ancient Roman prototype for our modern, velvety concoctions was cream mixed with berries and Alpine snow. The treat did not make it to America until the 1740s, when it appeared at the mansion of the governor of Maryland. It was being hawked publicly in New York by the year 1777; its first advertiser was an Italian confectioner, Philip Lenzi.

Once ensconced in the colonies, ice cream rapidly took off. George Washington was a big fan, as were Thomas Jefferson and Dolley Madison. By the first decades of the nineteenth century, the Italian background was being fused with a home-grown heritage. John Mariani notes that around that time the old expression "Neapolitan ice cream" was being challenged by "Philadelphia ice cream," which referred to a specifically American style of rich ice cream.

America's fascination with the dessert was much encouraged in 1846, with the invention of the portable, cranked ice cream freezer, and then again in 1904, with the appearance of the ice cream cone. Credit for this most American of ice cream paraphernalia goes to a vendor at that year's St. Louis World's Fair—the same fair that may have given us the hot dog. Which of the fifty ice cream sellers at that event first plopped his wares in a cone cannot be determined with any certainty. According to Paul Dickson, it was either a Syrian immigrant named Ernest Hamwi or another Italian, Italo Marchiony. Hamwi was a vendor of *zalabia,* a Persian-style waffle, which he offered to an ice cream vendor in the next booth when the latter ran out of dishes. Marchiony patented a pastry mold just a few months before the fair opened that produced "small round pastry cups with sloping sides."

COKE

It is not without reason that American intrusion into foreign economies in the 1960s was called "Cocacolonization" or that Pepsi executives grow apoplectic from their inability to portray "Coke" as merely a brand name and not the generic term for cola. Coke, which celebrated its hundredth birthday in 1986, is in every sense of the word a national institution.

That institution was created in 1886 by an Atlanta druggist named John S. Pemberton, who stirred up a syrup of coca leaves and cola nuts in his backyard and sold it in his own drugstore as a medicine. He experimented by adding soda water to the syrup, and expanded his distribution. In 1891 another pharmacist, Asa B. Candler, who had taken the elixir for headaches, acquired the rights to Pemberton's formula for the staggering sum of $2,000. Eight years later he set up the franchising system that is the basis of the company's success even today, and put the stuff into bottles. Ready to drink, its availability spreading coast to coast, Coke was on its way to becoming a multibillion dollar concern.

Various theories were advanced to account for the success of the product, including the tenacious old canard that the "cocaine" in it was addictive. But, as Waverley Root and Richard de Rochemont tell us, Coke's success has had much more to do with its skillful advertising, which, like all effective advertising, pushes the symbolic rather than the pragmatic value of the product. Anthropologist Sidney Mintz suggests that the appeal of the homey, good old-fashioned Coke is related to the "sociability of ingestion." The ads show happy peer groups repeatedly consuming Coke, and so "an illusory good fellowship is endlessly reimagined and reenacted." So Coke sells because, thanks to the ad department, consuming it makes us feel *loved*.

AMERICA'S CUP

Legend has it that America abruptly switched from tea to coffee on the morning after the Boston Tea Party. In fact, the colonists had been drinking both beverages for almost a hundred years, and it was coffee that had taken hold first. The first coffeehouse—that mainstay of seventeenth-century British intellectual life—had opened around 1670. The first Boston tearoom was licensed twenty years later. Both stimulants remained popular until George III's government refused to rescind the tea tax in 1770. If Americans switched to coffee during the American Revolution, it was not a long-lasting change. In the 1790s tea regained the lead, for the simple reason that it was cheaper. It was only during the War of 1812, when British tea became unavailable, that the changeover to coffee became permanent. The reason had as much to do with money as with pride. By the early 1800s the coffee bean, long the exclusive property of the East, had been imported into Brazil, and so for the first time the new nation could enjoy excellent coffee at a reasonable price.

KAFFEEKLATSCH

Klatschen in German means "to gossip." So, strictly speaking, a *kaffeeklatsch* is a gossip session at which coffee is served. The term arose in the early 1800s to describe a peculiarly middle class phenomenon: the gathering of German burgher wives in the cities of a rapidly urbanizing nation. According to the Pan-American Coffee Bureau, the males who coined the gently mocking term had as much reason to be uneasy as to be amused because *Hausfrauen* in the sophisticated cities regularly sharing their thoughts during a period characterized by radical ideas was potentially quite disruptive of wifely obedience. After all, British feminist Mary Wollstonecraft had published her *Vindication of the Rights of Women* in 1792 and French concepts of liberty and equality were still very much in the air.

It would be a mistake, I think, to imagine that what the women talked about was the emancipation of their sex. Even in the more liberal United States, women's rights did not become a hot issue until the 1840s, and German women did not get the vote until 1919. Yet group solidarity can be promoted even when it is not a topic on the official agenda, and it may not be an overstatement to say, in the Coffee Bureau's guarded phrasing, that the institution tracks "the progress of European woman from the time she began to share man's world of new ideas and, ultimately, to compete for her place in society."

RED WINE, RED MEAT

The traditional association of red wine with red meat and white wine with light meat and fish is based not on a simple color correspondence but on a principle of gustatory affinity. Red wines are thought to go better with red meat because, being robust themselves, they complement the meat's hearty taste. White wines are more suitable for lighter fare because they are subtler and more delicate. The principle is basically sound, because red wines are made with the skin of the grape and white wines are not. This is what gives red wines their color and, generally speaking, more body than the whites. But as with most principles, this one, too, must be qualified.

For one thing, some white wines *are* strong enough to stand up to the heartiest foods. One of the richest meals I have ever had—a Chinese banquet bursting with red meats—was accompanied by an "aggressive" white wine that complemented the flavors perfectly. For another thing, some "light" meats and fishes are so strongly flavored that most white wines would be overwhelmed by them. For example, the oily-fleshed fish of the Loire valley is traditionally prepared in red wine—and nobody complains about the colors. Moreover, in Paris it is customary to serve red wine with poultry.

Finally, there is the question of rosé. According to the strict color scheme, the only things to be served with this wine would be strawberry ice cream and boiled ham. Obviously, the Crayola approach to menu planning has its limits.

LETTING THE WINE BREATHE

A bottle of wine should be opened an hour or so before drinking it to allow any sediment in it to settle and to aerate it—that is, to let it absorb oxygen, or "breathe." Wine expert Raymond Wellington says this applies only to red wines and almost exclusively to those over ten years old. Letting last year's chablis "breathe," therefore, is an exercise in pretension.

Allowing sediment to settle is obviously a sound idea, unless you like the dregs clinging to your teeth. The advantage of oxygenation is more obscure. Apparently it improves the bouquet of some wines because it releases the esters, ethers, and aldehydes, which give the drink its particular "nose." That's why you decant wine before serving it and why you swirl wine before tasting it. Decanting is key here, because the whole point of removing the cork is to set up that air-ester exchange. But unless you also pour the wine out of its narrow-necked bottle into a wide-mouthed container, the amount of wine surface that can actually come in contact with the air will be negligible.

SNIFFING THE CORK

It is nearly pointless to sniff a cork that has just been removed from a wine bottle. As wine expert Raymond Wellington puts it, "It is the wine itself you want to smell. After all, a cork smells like a cork." What you are expected to do with the cork, when you are handed it by the sommelier, is to "check its condition and authenticity." An authentic cork has been placed in the bottle at its point of origin and will say, if it is French, *"Mis en bouteille dans nos caves."* As to condition, what you look for is moistness, which indicates that the wine has been stored properly (on its side), with the cork constantly wet and thus expanded, preventing the entry of air. A dry or crumbly cork indicates that air has very likely seeped in, which can damage the best of vintages. Of course, a moist cork is no guarantee of quality in itself, and the only defect you are likely to pick up from cork-sniffing is out-and-out vinegarization. Which is why you want to smell the wine.

WINE TASTING

According to the standard wine-tasting ritual, first you check out the color of the wine, then you hold the glass to your nose to ascertain the wine's bouquet, then you take a sip and swish it around in your mouth to determine its taste and general "feel"—and only then do you nod to the sommelier and say, "Thank you, Gaston, it fairly gallops with aplomb." The steps of this little scenario might seem labored unless you know that the true oenophile considers wine a satisfaction for many of the senses: Color is a treat for the eyes, the bouquet for the sense of smell, and the mouthful for both the sense of taste and, less obviously, the sense of touch. The "feel" of a wine is aptly named, even if it is your mouth doing the touching. The only sense missing from this tableau is the supposedly irrelevant sense of sound. Some suggest, however, that the pop of the cork delights the ears.

DRINKING A "TOAST"

From the days of ancient Greece to the 1700s, the custom of drinking
to someone's health was known as "drinking a health." William
Iversen notes that the Greeks at a typical banquet might drink a
health to every deity on Olympus, and that the Romans, never to be
exceeded in excess, often downed multiple healths to each other's
mistresses, sometimes drinking a cup of wine for each letter in the
favored belle's name.

The term *toast* replaced *health* in Restoration days, reportedly
because of an incident that took place in the English city of Bath.
As described by Richard Steele in a 1709 *Tatler,* a pair of young
blades had paused by one of that city's public baths to admire a
"celebrated Beauty" bathing therein. One dipped a glass in and,
following the Roman custom, which was appropriate for that most
Roman of British towns, drank a health to the fountain's fair occu-
pant. In England there was a 200-year-old custom of placing pieces
of spiced toast in one's wine. The health-giver's companion, acknowledging this custom, swore that "tho' he liked not the Liquor,
he would have the Toast." Thus was born the conceit of seeing the
person to whom a health was drunk as the toast (as in "toast of the
town"). Eventually *toast* also came to mean the act of proposing or
drinking a health and the words spoken in the toast's honor.

CLINKING GLASSES

George Stimpson (1948) provides two theories regarding the origin
of clinking glasses. The less probable theory dates the custom from
the late seventeenth and early eighteenth centuries, when English
sympathizers with the exiled Stuart royal family drank secret toasts
to their favorite by passing their glasses over finger bowls to indicate
that even though the words of the toast went to the sitting monarch,
their hearts were with the one "over the water." When finger bowls
were banished from English tables to discourage the practice, the
Stuart champions passed their glasses surreptitiously over each other
or touched them together in quick complicity.

The second, less tortuous explanation is that the custom is a
survivor of an ancient "mutual trust" ceremony. In the days of

frequent poisonings, even among "friends," drinkers would pour a little of their wine into each other's cups, to ensure that neither had it in for the other. Hence the touching of rims today.

DRINKING TO SEAL A DEAL

The custom of sealing a business agreement with drinks has an obvious and simple celebratory aspect that gives a basic sense of its appropriateness. When you have just transferred ownership of a multinational corporation, you want to endorse your good spirits about the deal with spirits of another kind. But you could do this just as well with a mutual meal, or a movie, or some form of exercise. Why don't folks who enjoy golf, for example, seal their bargains by playing nine holes?

The reason may have something to do with the ancient custom of toasting, and specifically with the act of clinking glasses: Drinking a beverage together may be a ritual announcement that you trust your new partner well enough to share a poisonable substance with him. A more likely explanation, I think, is that the custom recalls ancient libations poured out to the gods to ensure success (as, for example, at a ship launching). "Libation" comes from the Greek *leibein*, "to pour," meaning, first, a poured offering, originally a sacrificial one, and, second, an act of ceremonious drinking. The two meanings are clearly related, and the encoded message of drinking on a deal is probably "May we prosper in what we have signed." It's a kind of secular offering against misfortune.

COCKTAIL HOUR

Cocktails as such have been drunk since at least 1806. In that year an upstate New York newspaper defined a cocktail as a mixture of liquor, sugar, water and bitters. Such a mixture can be of great use, the paper said, to political candidates "because, a person having swallowed a glass of it, is ready to swallow anything else." The term gradually came to mean any alcoholic mixed drink, and by the end of the century its consumption had become dispersed throughout polite (and impolite) society.

But although drinking cocktails is quite old in this country, the idea of the cocktail hour is not. Lowell Edmunds identifies the Roaring Twenties as the creator of the drinks-before-dinner ritual, and points out that it was a direct result of the Volstead Act. People began drinking in their own homes because, after 1920, that was the only legal place they *could* drink. At that time, the cocktail hour was just that, one hour long—the designated sixty minutes between the arrival of one's guests and the formal sitting down to dinner. Gradually this "fortifying" period was extended, and after the repeal of Prohibition the cocktail "hour" became an event in itself. No longer a mere preliminary to dinner, it became a party in its own right—that ubiquitous twentieth-century phenomenon at which, in Judith Martin's malicious phrasing (1982), you get to meet "all the people your friends don't like well enough to invite to dinner."

As the length of the cocktail gathering grew, its venue broadened too, so that one began to take cocktails not only in the privacy of one's home but also, after Prohibition, in cocktail lounges (a creation of the 1930s), and eventually in plain, non-loungelike bars as well. Today we have come full circle, with the vast majority of stiff drinks being served, once again, away from home, during that predictably misnamed two-hour inebriation ceremony known as the "happy hour."

STIRRED, NOT SHAKEN

If there is a modern American version of the medieval search for the Holy Grail, it must be the search for the perfect martini. The praises of this elusive drink have been sung by champions as distinguished as M. F. K. Fisher, who claimed that a well-made martini had "more often been my true friend than any two-legged creature," and H. L. Mencken, who likened it to a sonnet. Encomiums like these suggest a spiritual aura to the drink, transcending its effectiveness as mere booze. Lowell Edmunds, in fact, emphasizes the quasi-religious aspects of martini drinking and goes so far as to call all that hullabaloo about chilled glasses and glass stirring rods and "whispers" of vermouth part of a nationally recognized "martini rite."

The facetiousness aside, Edmunds's analysis is on target. There is an undeniable liturgical feel to individual fanciers' personal recipes, and a clearly ceremonial cast to the instructions by which these snorts should be compounded. The martini is a drink that first must be mixed in a special vessel and then must be poured reverently into another special vessel to be drunk. The ratio of ingredients must be exactly 4 to 1, or 7 to 1, or 11 to 1, depending on the priest in charge of the mixing. The liquids, in earlier times shaken vigorously, now must always be stirred not shaken, preferably with a glass stirrer, and according to some aficionados always in the same direction. Consider also that the mixture must never be adulterated with water (Edmunds calls the martini on the rocks the "ultimate denial" of the classic mix) and that in European folklore the silver bullet is thought to be proof against werewolves, and it is not hard to conclude that in the American "silver bullet" mixing rite, we are dealing with an intoxication less physical than symbolic.

THE HORSEMEAT TABOO

Why don't Americans eat horsemeat? It's as nutritious and tasty as beefsteak and, in fact, is sometimes pawned off as such in cheap restaurants in France. Ancient people from Mongolia to northern Europe ate horseflesh, and in modern times it has been served sporadically, in such unlikely places as Paris cafes (during the 1870 siege of the Paris Commune) and the Harvard Faculty Club (during World War II). Frederick Simoons cites "familiarity with an animal" as a common rationale for a taboo, but this hardly suggests a rigid sanction. Farm families know their pigs and tom turkeys as intimately as they know their horses, yet they still end up as hamsteaks and drumsticks.

The American prejudice against horseflesh has little to do with the cowboy mentality or with the animal's usefulness. It harks back to a religious injunction that is well over a thousand years old. In 732, Pope Gregory III, realizing that horse-eating was a feature of the pagan Germans' religious rites, ordered the meat banned from Christian tables. This papal order was the beginning of the end for what had been a widespread practice.

According to Peter Farb and George Armelagos, the religious ban on the pagan food provided clerical sanction for "what had become an ecological necessity." Horse-eating makes sense when there are extensive grazing lands available for raising the animals, and only "so long as their usefulness for transportation, warfare, or agriculture is not outweighed by their consumption of domestic grain." These conditions ceased to be satisfied in Europe in the early Middle Ages; thus horse-eating, even without Gregory, was doomed.

The American repugnance for roasting horsemeat should be seen as a survivor of European bias. With North America's vast pastures, horses might well have been raised for food throughout our history and our cowboys might have followed the Mongolian horsemen's example of eating their mounts once they died. But the cultural bias, once set, proved too strong. Today, with the bias enforced by a thousand Westerns, we are as likely to start eating horses as we are to start eating cats and dogs.

"HOLD THE GRUBWORMS"

Why don't Westerners eat insects? They provide a wide range of texture and taste, they're plentiful, and they pack as much protein to the inch as almost everything else that we eat except steak. The standard, barroom explanations are transparent. "They don't taste good" is a meaningless proscription unless you feel that "taste" is somehow innate. The experience of the vast majority of *Homo sapiens,* who have been munching them since the Pleistocene, says that insects can be quite yummy. The objection that insects are dirty is also specious. Insects are no more dirty—that is, enmired in soil or attractive to germs—than any other type of living creature, and they're a lot cleaner than pigs or chickens, which we consume with nary a thought about contagion. Yet it's true that we see insects as "yucky." Why?

Since most of the world's people do eat insects, a theory that attempts to explain our abhorrence must be oriented to "nurture," not "nature." That is, insect hatred must be learned, not inherited. One theory that proceeds from this bias, and that presents a good rationale for our behavior, is that of optimal foraging. As explained by Marvin Harris (1985), optimal foraging theory says that human beings tend to maximize their caloric intake and that they will forage for, and injest, only those foods that will give them the greatest caloric return per hour of invested time. If you spend three hours

putting a squirrel into a pot and four hours for an equivalent-sized
marmoset, it makes sense to concentrate on squirrels. Insects are
avoided in certain cultures, Harris says, because, although they are
edible enough in the abstract, the time it takes to gather and stew
them makes them an inefficient food source compared to protein-
concentrating animals such as pigs and cattle. Where you don't have
pork and beef in abundance, people naturally gravitate to grub-
worms. In the highly carnivorous, barnyard-teeming West, it makes
no sense to devour forty earthworms when, for the same expenditure
of energy, you can down a sixteen-ounce steak.

GUM CHEWING

Mexican dictator Antonio Lopez de Santa Anna left two legacies to
the United States. One was the rallying cry "Remember the Alamo,"
which was indirectly instrumental in making Texas our twenty-
eighth state. The other was chewing gum. Exiled to, of all places,
Staten Island in the 1860s, Santa Anna eased the tensions of his
forced retirement by chewing on pieces of chicle, the latex sap of the
sapodilla tree, which Central American Indians had been masticat-
ing since Aztec times. When he left New York, he left behind a large
chunk of the stuff, which Thomas Adams, a neighbor, discovered.
After trying unsuccessfully to turn the chicle into rubber, Adams
sold it to a candy store in New Jersey. At a time when tobacco
chewing was ubiquitous in America, the novel "chaw" caught on
quickly, and the U.S. gum industry was born.

That industry was controlled by Adams and his descendants almost to the end of the century, when the lead was gradually wrested
from them by an energetic Chicago salesman named William Wrigley, Jr. According to the Wrigley Company press office, the founder
of the giant gum concern came to Chicago in 1891 with thirty-two
dollars in his pocket and got into the chewing gum business incidentally, by offering gum as a premium with baking powder. The premium "seemed more promising than the product it was supposed to
promote," and young Wrigley wisely shifted gears. Relying on the
innovative use of dealer premiums and extensive advertising (still
rare in those days), he unseated the established "chewing gum trust"
and made himself king of the jawboners. Today his company markets

a dozen different kinds of gum, including its original, 1893 winner, Juicy Fruit.

Even before the Wrigley phenomenon, chewing was traditionally American. Colonists had copied the New England Indian custom of chewing spruce gum even before the 1800s, and after about 1850 the chewing of paraffin also became popular. So the Santa Anna–Adams–Wrigley combine merely capitalized on an established fad.

Why gum chewing should be so popular here is open to question. Given the usefulness of chewing as a means of relieving tension, our addiction to the habit may suggest something about the neurosis level of American society. Waverley Root and Richard de Rochemont, pointing to the instant, if ersatz, nourishment provided by the habit, suggest that gum chewing, like its progenitor twig-chewing, may be a sign of dietary deficiency. And the custom also has some obvious socializing effects. Especially among teenagers, the exchange of gum sticks functions as a kind of barter system, redistributing wealth even as it communalizes interactions. At the same time, the blatant chewing of gum, often in violation of authority, serves as a badge of identity—chewing gum (with or without bubbles) acts as a kind of secret jaw shake among intimates.

TIPPING

There are two common explanations for the origin of tipping. The *Oxford English Dictionary* says *tip* was seventeenth-century underworld slang for "give"—as in "Tip me your wallet or your life." Opponents of tipping will probably prefer this explanation, since it suggests the practice was originally a form of theft. A less reputable, but nonetheless charming, explanation is that in Renaissance coffeehouses, boxes were set near the door, into which customers could drop gratuities: these boxes, according to the story, bore the legend "To Insure Promptitude," which was ultimately shortened to TIP. Whether it was an enterprising serving wench or a proprietor with his eye on depressing wages who first thought up the idea, the story does not say.

Tipping became common in England by the middle of the eighteenth century. Because it is ill suited to a country without an established servant class, it did not catch on in America until after the

Civil War, when former slaveholders suddenly found themselves having to pay the help and when nouveau riche Northern industrialists adopted the European fashion as part of conspicuous display. By the turn of the century, we had made the custom our own, and the stereotypical American "big tipper" was on his way.

Today, although the lines between protection money, bribery, and thanks for services rendered remain as fuzzy as ever, tipping has become universal, not least because, in an increasingly uncertain economy, it provides the growing service class with income that is at least as reliable as wages and that is less susceptible to tax review. Not surprisingly, government officials number among the few diehards who still question the tipping system. They have a point too. Tippers International estimates that U.S. workers rake in about $5 billion a year in tips. The taxes on that amount, if all of it were reported, could make the down payment on a hammer for the Pentagon.

DIETING

With literally hundreds of diet books now in print in the United States, it makes sense to ask why a people of plenty are so fanatical about losing weight. The standard explanation for the thinness craze is that dieting is good for your health. On close examination this is suspect. True, obesity is not good for your health, but neither is the purge-and-binge syndrome that so often accompanies modern dieting, and some health authorities now counsel that remaining just slightly overweight may be easier in the long run on the metabolism than a swing cycle of starvation and stuffing. So there is more to weight reduction than good health. I would suggest appearance, penance, and conspicuous display as three additional factors.

First, concern for appearance is especially common among women, who buy the majority of diet books. There is nothing particularly strange about folks dropping poundage to appear sexier. It is only important to point out that the desire to starve oneself into irresistibility reflects not so much the image of an ideal body type as it does the male view of women as helpless. The current anorexic ideal is a replication of the nineteenth-century cadaver look—the wasp waists, pale complexions, and limp wrists that fed the swooning vogue and that, then as now, promoted the idea of woman as a delicate creature needing physical as well as monetary support from the man.

Second, since dieting is hard, disagreeable work, there may be an element of expiation involved. As a nation we are prone to obesity because of our natural abundance. Perhaps the diet craze reflects a national confession that we have sinned by overindulging for so long. Third World people often hate Americans precisely because we have so much to eat. Perhaps dieting reflects a corresponding self-hatred and an attempt to make amends by cutting calories.

Third, the flip side of the penance explanation is that people may diet ostentatiously, as a way of demonstrating that they *can.* In an economy where the cheapest foods are usually the fattiest, dieting necessarily taxes the pocketbook more strenuously than would wolfing down burgers and fries. Weight Watchers and Le Menu frozen dinners are pricier than Mrs. Swanson's more caloric fare, and we should not discount the status attraction of being able to afford upscale trimmers. It may not be accidental that two of the most popular diets of recent years—the Scarsdale Diet and the Beverly Hills Diet—were named after luxury neighborhoods.

ALL THROUGH THE HOUSE:

FAMILY AFFAIRS

"KISS IT AND MAKE IT BETTER"

Since there is no obvious medical benefit to be derived from a kiss, the common parental habit of kissing a child's injury to make it go away seems to be purely psychological. It makes both parent and child *feel* better. The practice may be a survivor of the primitive custom of "sucking out evil," in which a shaman or other healer orally withdraws infection from the afflicted part of a patient's body. Except in those cases where actual poison is sucked out (for example, snakebite venom), the curative effect may be the same psychological one whether the procedure takes place in the African bush or in Des Moines.

Not that the psychological effect is negligible. In spite of the cause-and-effect bias of Western medicine, it has been demonstrated many times that the panacea effect is more than mental. When a patient *believes* in a cure, there is a much greater chance that it will work, even when the cure is medically groundless. Thus kissing the place to make it better, like the witch doctor's evil-sucking gambit, can sometimes give the patient the mental confidence that will hasten the body's own healing process. There is no reason to believe that this procedure is any less reliable than the modern hospital's armory of sugar pills.

TOOTHBRUSHING

The hygienic reasons for toothbrushing have a special point in a culture such as ours, where addiction to sugar is epidemic. But this custom is by no means universal. The ancient Romans used toothpicks and rinsed their mouths with urine instead of brushing three times a day. Many Asian peoples chew betel nuts. And many peoples do nothing at all.

Toothbrushing should therefore be seen not as a "natural" custom but as the peculiar behavior of some Western tribes. Horace Miner took this relativist view in an engaging anthropological spoof a generation ago. In discussing the "body ritual" of a North American group he called the "Nacirema," he depicted our obsessive teeth cleansing as a culture-specific "mouth rite," consisting of "inserting a small bundle of hog hairs into the mouth, along with certain magical powders, and then moving the bundle in a highly formalized series of gestures." In addition to performing this private mouth rite, Miner said, the Nacirema also pay regular visits to a "holy-mouth-man" who drills holes in their teeth and fills them with supernatural substances, in order to "arrest decay and draw friends." "The extremely sacred and traditional character of the rite is evident in the fact that the natives return to the holy-mouth-men year after year, despite the fact that their teeth continue to decay." If "ritual" is a stylized, repetitive behavior designed to ensure protection, Miner's spoof may make sense as well as fun.

THE TOOTH FAIRY

Primitive peoples believe that hair, nail clippings, and lost teeth remain magically linked to the owner even after they have been disconnected from his body. As any voodoo artist will tell you, if you want to grind someone into powder, you don't need to touch him at all. It's quite enough to stomp on a missing molar and let "contagious magic" do the rest. This is why peoples all over the world traditionally hide lost body parts, lest they fall into the wrong hands.

American children's ritual of hiding lost teeth under their pillows probably derives distantly from this practice. But there is an obvious difference, for when Suzie conceals her baby bicuspid, she fully expects it to be found, and by a good magician, not an evil one. Moreover, she expects to be paid for having surrendered it, and at the going rate. Nothing more clearly suggests the blithe commercial gusto of our culture than this transformation of a fearful superstition into a cheery business transaction.

Because American children expect fair exchange for their lost teeth, it is likely that the tooth fairy ritual derives more immediately from the European, and particularly German, tradition of placing a lost tooth in a mouse or a rat hole. The folk belief governing this practice is that when a new tooth grows in, it will possess the dental qualities, not of the original, lost tooth, but of whatever creature finds it, so the creatures of choice would be those world-class chompers, the rodents.

Thus the optimistic, "fair exchange" principle most likely started in Germany and was brought here by German immigrants. It was only left to America to replace the beneficent "tooth rat" with the more agreeable fairy and to replace the traditional hope of hard molars with our more characteristic hope of hard cash.

COUNTING-OUT RHYMES

The social function of counting-out rhymes is to introduce an element of civility into what might otherwise be a mad grab for the ball: formulas like "Eenie, Meenie, Miney, Moe" and "Engine, Engine" thus organize play by establishing a ground-level consensus about procedure before the game begins. The fly in this formalizing social glue is the possibility for chooser manipulation—the fact that a clever chooser, foreseeing where the rhyme will end, can adjust his "random" starting point so that certain players are eliminated. But that is a necessary evil for the game to begin at all. There are, unfortunately, parallels here to the way adults play geopolitics: one reason that wars take so long to negotiate to a conclusion is that grown children play counting-out games to determine the shape of the table.

DISHWASHING

Way back in 1950, James Brossard and Eleanor Boll pointed out "the family separation caused by modern techniques and ways of living" and called the formal dishwashing "rite" of modern America "the single opportunity" remaining for family-shared work responsibility. Although this was a bit of an exaggeration, with the increasing availability of extramural entertainment for children and with the consequent decline of the home as what sociologists call an "activity center," such minor chores as dishwashing indeed have become communalizing rituals. They are appropriate to this end because they involve a well-defined set of discrete steps, each of which can be performed by a single actor, and because all the actors must cooperate in order to get through the entire operation effectively. In the dishwashing ritual, the washer, the dryer, and the "putter-away-er" must all do their parts in a prescribed fashion, or the ritual cannot be completed. Obviously this structure does more than teach the virtues of cooperation. It also provides a kitchen-sized model of the culture's fundamental mode of production, that of division of labor and the assembly line. Whatever their feelings about each other and about the job, the members of an efficient dishwashing team learn to distance themselves from those feelings in order to get the job done. In this sense the family is preparation, not abstractly for life, but for what Marxists call the alienated labor of industrialism.

SIBLING RIVALRY

Bickering among siblings is so common in our culture that it is normally thought of as "natural" competition for parental love. It may also be an enculturated response, not to family life in general, but to specific parameters of the modern family. Sibling rivalry is likely to become a conventionalized method of adapting to fraternal or sororal stress in situations where two conditions apply.

First, sibling rivalry might arise where kinship is narrowly defined as applying to the immediate family only. In the old-fashioned, extended family, ties of affection were understood to apply to a wide circle of distant relations, and this diffusion of kinship links may have made it easier for children to manage their feelings of competitiveness. Forced closeness, whether in rats or in humans, tends to breed resentment and frustration. Possibly the prevalence of sibling rivalry in our culture has something to do with the "nucleation" of family life, and with the related fact that family size tends to be fairly small. It may be easier to feel resentment toward your rivals when there are only two of them than when there are ten or fifteen.

Second, sibling rivalry may increase in the absence of formal inheritance customs. In many of the old extended families, the rule of succession was primogeniture. The eldest (and generally the eldest son) was assumed to be the appropriate recipient of most of the parents' wealth and attention. Although not a fair system, it may have tended toward more stability, since the inequality had the force of tradition. In our more egalitarian family structure, tension is bound to arise because the "rules" of sibling priority are not as well defined. Hence sibling rivalry, in a democratic culture, may be seen as a revolution of changing expectations.

THE WEEKLY ALLOWANCE

In the late Middle Ages, many husbands gave their wives silver pins as a traditional New Year's present. Eventually this custom gave way to the presentation of "pin money" instead. Pin money in turn was transformed into a yearly or other periodic "allowance" for domestic expenses and small luxuries. The modern allowances for children reflect the same type of arrangement, but they are peculiar in three ways. First, the very fact that parents give allowances to their children, rather than their spouses, suggests an important shift in domestic focus. A society that gives its children pin money would have been unthinkable in the Middle Ages. Second, that these allowances are thought of as covering entertainment rather than expenses suggests the opening out of possibilities for youngsters in a fluid, externally oriented culture. "Here's your weekly movie money" is a very different proposition from, "Here's enough for this month's groceries." Finally, the fact that allowances are typically given—although not so acknowledged—in exchange for services rendered ("Do your chores or no allowance this week") suggests the extent to which even the simplest familial relations have become mercantilized. Indeed, the modern child's management of the weekly allowance often serves as an early model of later money management. Thus, as pin money changes from gift to transaction, one learns from a very early age to be a member of the market economy.

BEDTIME STORIES

Parents who read their young children stories before sleep are maintaining the last vestige of a family reading tradition that, until the advent of radio, was a principal form of nightly entertainment in many homes. In Puritan times children were subjected to a period of Bible reading in the early evening, and in the more secular eighteenth and nineteenth centuries, the nightly texts were taken from "the classics"—meaning anything from Vergil to Dickens. The radio revolution early in this century introduced the novelty of the disembodied voice as well as a range of serial stories and sound effects that few parents could compete with. So "reading time" audiences diminished until it was only the younger children who were still innocent enough to appreciate the one-to-one attention of their parents reading to them. At the same time, abridged versions of the classics (with the "dull parts" taken out) appeared, and publishers turned more and more attention to short-format, heavily illustrated stories that a parent and child could read together, with the pictures doing a good deal of the work. In the age of television, of course, this pictorialization was essential as a way of competing with the visual medium.

AN APPLE FOR THE TEACHER

The custom of schoolchildren presenting an apple to the teacher has pretty much gone the way of the double feature and the dunking stool. Too bad. In these days of Apple IIs in every classroom, the occasional gift of a piece of fruit would be a welcome reminder of the era when education was one-on-one and when good teaching meant firing up your students' minds rather than identifying their percentile rankings.

As for the origin of the custom, it obviously contains an element of bribery—a prepayment for services expected. You offer sweet fruit to authority figures to sweeten their dispositions—and thus make the disposition of your grades more predictable. But the custom might also be explained as a vestige of payment in kind. In the early days of public education, schoolteachers were not always salaried. Often they would be paid in goods and services, and the presentation of fresh produce, especially in a farm community, would be a perfectly legitimate form of payment. An apple for the teacher may be a survivor of this arrangement.

CRAMMING FOR EXAMS

This last-minute approach to studying speaks not so much to American anti-intellectualism as to a peculiarity of the American education system known as "continuous assessment." Under this system, educators assume that students cannot enjoy studying and that they therefore must be constantly monitored (with quizzes, midterms, and finals). This assumption becomes a self-fulfilling prophecy, because when you know you're going to be tested every three or four weeks, it's easy to organize the entire term's work around these critical "judgment points." Since it's not impossible to "learn" four weeks of data in one night, students who care primarily about passing tests become involved in their own education only in this feast-and-famine pattern.

The European system of higher education typically does not involve continuous assessment, and this leads to a very different outcome. In many European universities, students are tested at the end of one year, and sometimes at the end of an entire course of study, which may take two or three years. European students, who have both more political power and more social respect than do American students, are not subjected to an insulting barrage of pop quizzes because they are assumed to be adults. And a good many of them behave like adults; realizing that cramming alone will not be sufficient to pass a year-end exam, they take their education as a long-term process, studying as they go. When you have only one chance to pass, you take that chance very seriously.

TEEN PHONE LINES

The separate phone line for teenagers is an outgrowth of the extension phone that was popular with baby boomers in the 1950s and that enabled Ma Bell to make millions off a generation of American "princesses." For parents and the phone company, the private line, like the old Princess model, seems an advance in both personal and social terms. But the technology has its down side. The negotiating ability that a one-phone family is obliged to develop cannot be developed as effectively when there is an alternate outside line. Thus the teenager's private line circumvents rather than addresses family communication binds. At the same time, although less obviously, the extra line decreases contact between teenagers and their friends. Why walk three blocks to be with a friend when you can "reach out and touch" him long distance? Thus the private line, like the CB radio and the automobile, actually inhibits the greater contact it promises.

THE SUNDAY DRIVE

People were going for Sunday drives long before there were automobiles, but the nature of the event in the good old days was less hectic and, in a sense, more theatrical. As James Bossard and Eleanor Boll indicate, the Sabbath drive in the horse-and-carriage era tended to be an "open show of family pride to well-known neighbors." It was an opportunity for families in small communities to display their latest finery (surrey fringe, Sunday suits) to each other and to do some visiting in the process. With the advent of the automobile, the options for the family outing were greatly expanded, and the traditional drive around town gave way to a more leisurely and less ostentatious excursion into the countryside. Then, in the 1950s, came the interstate highway system, which sent the Sunday outing custom into its final, and most frenetic, phase.

With the availability of superhighways, Americans were suddenly afforded the option not simply of driving as an end in itself but of driving in order to *get* somewhere, and fast. It was suddenly possible to spend the day as a tourist in another state and still be back for the children's bedtime. As a result, what had begun as a way of being seen became a hellbent-for-leather method of seeing, of visiting far-flung relations, of checking off items on an inventory.

COUPON-CLIPPING

A woman walks into a supermarket, buys $130 worth of groceries, hands the clerk a $10 bill and a wad of manufacturer's cents-off coupons, and ends up with $3 change. Sound like a fantasy? It actually happened, just as described, to "coupon queen" Susan Samtur on a shopping trip with consumer advocate Betty Furness. Although the savings on this particular trip were unusually high, the possibility of what Samtur calls "cashing in at the checkout" is real. By religiously buying only name-brand items (they're the ones that offer reduction coupons), spending a few minutes each day updating your coupon files, planning each shopping trip in advance to take advantage of the coupons you have, and focusing on stores that offer "double coupons" (a price reduction of twice the coupon's face value), dedicated couponers cut down their food costs dramatically. Samtur says she cuts her weekly shopping bill approximately in half by using coupons.

You might see the couponing craze as a kind of underground, alternate economy—a citizens' response to inflation. Couponing, supported by a network of newsletters like Samtur's own *Refundle Bundle,* is a consumerist endeavor, but its principal beneficiaries are still the businesses that offer the deals. Ever since the C. W. Post cereal company issued the first penny-off coupon back in 1895, coupons have functioned as a loss-leader investment in attracting customers and in building brand loyalty with temporary inducements. Samtur herself describes them as "the most visible and most widely distributed promotional scheme in the industry's whole bag of tricks." Whether or not you use coupons (and four out of five Americans do, at least occasionally), may depend less on how much time you are willing to devote to making this hobby pay off than on how closely you wish your food consumption to be tied in to the agribusiness network.

TAG SALES

Whether they're called tag sales, yard sales, garage sales, or lawn sales, these examples of private enterprise at the grass-roots level indicate not only the need, in any highly organized economy, for alternate methods of distribution but also the creativity that local networks can bring to bear on that need. The immense attraction of the tag sale has to do with more than low prices—although being able to buy a fifty-dollar sports jacket for three dollars is no small incentive. It has to do with a nostalgia for community—both in terms of interpersonal relations and in terms of simple, barterlike trade—that modern society has all but expunged. And it has to do with a populist resentment of government and of the business community it so often serves.

Only one or two of the hundreds of garage sales I have attended displayed the local government's fee-paid permit sticker. And none of the sellers collected sales tax. This should come as no surprise. Tag sales represent a form of economy that precedes both government and capitalist enterprise. It is an economy of redistribution rather than profit, in which the actors, buyers and sellers alike are "just folks" and in which the prospect of cleaning out the cellar is more important than taking someone to the cleaners. To the members of the tag sale economy, modest gains are quite necessary, but they are also sufficient. It is because of the system's low profit margin and the social difficulties of collaring "folks" in their own front yards that governments ignore the tax dodge and blink at the lack of permits. Thus the tag sale phenomenon, like other examples of underground markets, represents a permissible flaunting of individualism.

TUPPERWARE PARTIES

Earl S. Tupper was a New England salesman who created two American institutions: a versatile plastic called poly-T, from which Tupperware products are made, and the Tupperware party, at which housewives serving as company "hostesses" display and sell the products to their friends. Tupper invented both in the 1940s, when World War II was already demonstrating the versatility of plastics. His company took off in the 1950s, as thousands of GIs were resettled in suburbia to become members of the consumer society. Tupper's luck was to happen upon poly-T when a woman could still afford to stay home and when her fondest desire (so the postwar magazines told her) was to have an up-to-date, "convenience" kitchen. His genius was to carry word-of-mouth advertising to its logical extreme by making satisfied customers his sole distributors.

The party concept was a stroke of brilliance. It both fueled and disguised the American enchantment with material goods by redefining an essentially economic affair as a form of neighborhood entertainment. Unlike the anonymous store setting, the Tupperware party is personal, interactive, subtly competitive—and fun. It is no wonder that in the Eisenhower years, when keeping up with the Joneses became a secular religion, the Yankee innovator's business skyrocketed.

RIDGEPOLE TREES

In the days of tract houses and thirty-day construction contracts, you don't see as many of them as you used to, but in rural areas of the United States, and especially in regions settled by Germans, when a new house is going up, you can still see small evergreen trees on the ridgepole, swaying in the wind like whimsical steeples. The similarity with steeples has some point, for trees have had a magical, religious significance to northern Europeans from ancient times, and numerous examples of early European tree worship have been documented. The placement of an evergreen tree at the peak of a new house reflects not only the awe that early peoples must have felt at the survival of these trees' foliage during winter but also their fear that, if not propitiated, the spirits of the wood that had been cut down to make the house would hinder or curse the construction. Thus, giving a representative tree pride of place, while the work was still going on, was a way of ensuring good luck.

KITCHEN WITCHES

Novelty shops in recent years have been selling small dolls called "kitchen witches," to be hung in that room as good luck charms. Given the dominant view of witches in North American culture—as unattractive, evil old crones—this might seem ironic or inappropriate. But kitchen witches, aside from being astride the traditional broomstick, are closer in appearance to Eastern European grandmothers than to the villainesses of popular legend. They don't wear black robes and cone hats, but bright-colored aprons and babushkas. Thus "witch" may be mildly satiric, and the good-luck aspects of the figures appropriate to their grandmotherly station.

Indeed, as feminist scholars have been pointing out for a decade, the women whom male clerics called witches, and whom they murdered by the hundreds throughout the centuries, probably *were* grandmotherly types: babushka-clad and quite at home in the kitchen. In the Middle Ages, an old woman with a knowledge of herbs, as useful in medicine as in cooking, might easily have been seen as a witch because she practiced the "black art" of healing; Latin American Spanish preserves the confusion today, in the word *bruja,* which means both "healer" and "witch." So the placement of a "witch" in a modern kitchen may evoke this centuries-old connection.

SPRING CLEANING

There is both a practical and a symbolic reason for doing a major housecleaning in the spring. The practical reason is that you *can.* With frost on the windows and ice on the steps, one's domestic zeal naturally tends to hibernate, often resulting in an accumulation of dust and debris throughout the winter months. With the advent of warmer weather, it's possible to open the windows without risking frostbite, and to start sweeping out the gathered bits of three months. The symbolic reason is that in the ancient agricultural and astronomical calendars, spring was the beginning of the year. We sweep our houses out around March 21, the date of the vernal equinox, for the same reason that we make noise on the night of December 31: to make it uncomfortable for the spirits of the old year to hang around and bedevil the new. Spring cleaning provides a psychological lift because it is a ritual of renewal, providing a symbolic break with the past and a welcoming in of the new season.

DOGS AND CATS

Although conspicuous ownership and status-seeking may have a great deal to do with pet ownership and the pet industry—whether you have a mutt or a Shar Pei, a Siamese or an alley cat—economics and display are only part of it. Studies of people who live alone show that those with pets live longer, and the lowering of blood pressure has been linked to the physical act of stroking one's pet.

On the more cynical side, Kathleen Szasz links people's obsession with dogs and cats to their inability to love other humans. This would explain the overwhelming popularity of pet dogs, since they are notoriously affectionate to their masters and they never care whom you flirted with last night.

The particular penchant for dogs and cats goes back many thousands of years. The dog was domesticated first, perhaps as early as 20,000 B.C. and certainly no later than 10,000 B.C. Some paleontologists suggest that, since the animal is a scavenger, it may have adopted humans rather than vice versa, although most surmise that *Homo sapiens* was the initiator of the relationship, because of the animal's potential usefulness. Maria Leach (1961) itemizes the dog's uses—as food, as a hunting companion, as a scavenger, as a watchdog, as a "friend"—in terms suggesting that the symbiosis between humans and *Canis canis* hasn't changed much over time, except that, unlike our Mesolithic forebears, we don't eat the animals.

Cats were domesticated only a little later than dogs, probably around 9000 B.C., the time of the transition from a nomadic, hunter-gatherer life style to that of crop-based village life. Although the Egyptians of later times worshipped the cat (and, less notoriously, the dog), the most likely reason for feline domestication is, again, that of usefulness: with the introduction of grain stores along with farming, the cat would have been an extra hand to help keep hungry rodents out of the food.

TRIMMING LAWNS

The well-trimmed lawn became an emblem of social respectability during the 1950s; it was in that expansive and status-conscious decade that Americans, newly suburbanized, rediscovered "the land" and immediately began, as their Puritan forebears had done, to subdue and "improve" it. In that era status-seeking merged with an older and deeper American rage for busyness, for control of nature, and for "progress." The lawn of the 1950s, no less than the fenced and manicured cornfield of the 1650s, expressed a national hunger to put wilderness in its place.

That hunger may have been inherited indirectly from the French, whose intoxication with regularity created Europe's most famous formal gardens in the seventeenth century. It is hard to imagine the immense lawns of Versailles being trimmed with a scythe, but the French passion for neatness required just that until the introduction, in the 1830s, of the horse-drawn lawn mower. The modern lawn mower, of course, has made cutting grass, as the advertisements would say, "almost a pleasure," and has made all but inconceivable the idea of a "good neighbor" with crabgrass shoots.

ARE WE HAVING FUN YET?:

ENTERTAINMENT

BASEBALL AS THE NATIONAL GAME

According to the inaugural issue of *The Ball Players' Chronicle,* published on June 6, 1867, the sport that was known as "the National game" at that time had in the 1850s been known as "the New York game." This is fitting, because ball clubs from New York City and its environs transformed the English game of rounders into what we now know as baseball. If anyone should be called the father of American baseball, it is New York banker Alexander Cartwright, who in the 1840s, as a leader of the Knickerbocker Base Ball Club, devised the core of the modern set of rules and helped to publicize the game nationwide. (Fellow New Yorker Abner Doubleday had nothing to do with its genesis, and the myth of his Cooperstown brainstorm got started only after the turn of the century.) The designation National game very likely originated in the fact that the earliest organized league, formed in 1859, was called the National Association of Base Ball Players.

But the sport has "national" as well as "National" features, and it is these that sustain its popularity. Chief among these elements is the ironic balance in baseball between starring roles and group solidarity. In most team sports, the emphasis is necessarily on cooperation; even the superstars on soccer and basketball teams are valuable chiefly as team players. In baseball the stress is far more visibly on the individual, and specifically on the confrontation between the batter and the pitcher; the attention of spectators is focused most of the time on these two principals. Baseball is thus perfectly suited to be the most popular pastime in a culture in which "doing your own thing" is a fetish. It is an ideal sport for a ruggedly individualistic society that pays lip service to the idea of community but retains its strongest kudos for the loner.

THE OPENING-DAY PITCH

Baseball has so long and so vociferously been touted as the American national game that it is not surprising to find our head of state wobbling out each new season's opening pitch. This minor spectacle, in addition to reestablishing the connection between Babe Ruth and the Founding Fathers, enables the opening-day crowd to compare the presidential arm with those of its favorite mound jockeys. It allows the crowd to convince itself, if only for a moment, that the guy in the White House is just folks. Patriotism, democracy, public farce—it's all there in the season's first ball.

The first first ball was thrown out in 1910, sixty-five years after New York's Knickerbocker Club laid down the game's basic rules, and nine years before the Black Sox scandal, in which Chicago threw the World Series to Cincinnati. In that relatively innocent era, the president was William Howard Taft, who in spite of his girth was well-suited to start the tradition. He had played enthusiastically as a boy, and he evidently believed, as all Americans were then raised to believe, that baseball was as close to pure sport as was possible this side of the Olympics. In his rich history of baseball, Harold Seymour quotes Taft: Baseball, he said, "summons to its presence everybody who enjoys clean, straight athletics." Taft threw out the first ball on April 4, in a game between Washington and Philadelphia that drew a then-record crowd of twelve thousand.

THE NATIONAL ANTHEM AT BALL GAMES

Although Francis Scott Key's "Star-Spangled Banner" was not officially made the American national anthem until 1931, by that time it had already served for decades as a popular patriotic air. Key's famous lyrics, set to the tune of an old English drinking song, were inspired by the British siege of Fort McHenry during the War of

1812. The stirring recognition at the end of the first stanza that "our flag was still there" gave the song wide appeal in the nineteenth century, especially in the military. The Union Army adopted it informally during the Civil War, and the U.S. Army officially embraced it in World War I.

The tradition of playing the song before athletic events, especially baseball games, was born, like the anthem itself, of wartime patriotism. According to the National Baseball Hall of Fame, the first evidence that a band had played the "national air" at a game appeared in *Sporting News* on April 19, 1917. It is probably not coincidental that, less than two weeks before, the United States had declared war on Germany. The practice was intermittent in the 1920s and 1930s, when few ball parks had public-address systems and when full-scale bands would have been hired only for special occasions. The opening anthem seems to have become standard practice in the early 1940s, when electronic advances allowed soloists to replace the more expensive bands, and when patriotism was again running high.

THE TV SHRINE

The ancient Romans placed small shrines within their homes for the worship of household gods. These shrines enabled them to establish connections between the mundane activities of Pompeii or Brindisium and the more exotic comings and goings of the deities. Gregor Goethals provides an interesting analysis of television as a similar kind of household shrine. Sitting in front of our private "video altars," he suggests, we are able to establish connections not just with the semisupernatural beings who inhabit Southfork Ranch and Knots Landing, but also with actual, distant events that, precisely because they come to us through the altar, take on "sacred" characteristics. Events such as the landing on the moon, or the funeral of a national hero, or the frenzied celebrations of Super Sunday become sacred events to the degree that they are beamed through to us via the Tube. Goethals says television, especially in its presentation of iconic images in its commercials, has become a "substitute for sacraments."

TV WRESTLING

It does not take very close attention to television wrestling to conclude that Hulk Hogan and his buddies are not wrestlers but performing acrobats—in other words, actors. The type of acting they do is highly, broadly stylized—full of blowsy oratory and stage winking. Gerald Craven and Richard Moseley point out that this makes TV wrestling a close cousin to melodrama. What these "actors on the canvas stage" do is exactly what the Handsome Harrys and Evil Landlords of a simpler era did. They enact a morality play in which pure virtue is pitted against pure vice. The ostensibly chaotic world of the wrestling ring is actually ruled by very tight conventions; for example, the initiation of unfair action by the villain, the use of illegal props, the "rescue" of a double-teamed "good guy" by his partner. These make the overall action quite predictable, even if (as is often the case today) "evil" is allowed to triumph in the short run. Thus the wrestling fan who follows the career of a favorite hero (or antihero) over time may get the same cathartic comfort, the same sense that the play will come out "all right," that nineteenth-century audiences were able to get in a single evening of melodrama.

SKIING STATUS

"There was a time," John Allen laments in an article on the origins of skiing, "when you did not have to lay out $250 for a pair of skis, $35 for poles, $250 for boots and up to $500 for clothing before you even got to the skiing slope." That time, he notes, passed about a hundred years ago, when manufacturers of sporting equipment began to push skiing as a fad for high society. From about 1825, when Norwegian immigrants introduced skiing into the American Midwest, to the turn of the century, the sport remained exclusively a Scandinavian pastime. It was part of a "winter culture" in which most skiers made their own skis, and in which skiing meant either cross-country trekking or ski jumping, not the downhill form so popular today. As winter country houses became popular, skiing gradually emerged as "an amusement for the middle class," and the foundations were laid for ski lodges, ski bunnies, and lift tickets. This last innovation—a creation of commercialized, multislope resorts—

reflects the increasing upscaling of the sport. Skiiers who have just returned from Killington or Gstaad keep their lift tickets dangling from their jackets for the same reason that Gilded Age ocean travelers kept port-of-call labels on their steamer trunks. They are advertisements not so much of their vacation experience, but of the social standing that the experience implies.

TURKEY SHOOTS

Mitford Mathews defines a turkey shoot as a "shooting match at which turkeys serve as targets and prizes." The development of this peculiarly American entertainment, from its heyday in the nineteenth century to its survival in many rural areas today, demonstrates the extent to which marketing structures have altered traditional recreational customs.

The original turkey shoots were popular gobbler-hunting parties of the last century, examples of sportsmanship gone batty that rivaled the Great Plains buffalo slaughters in their excess. Thanks to enclosure hunts (in which the birds were surrounded by a ring of hunters and pressed to their deaths in the center) and to roost shoots (in which hunters, often at night, felled hundreds of birds from their perches), the wild turkey population of North America, already being decimated by habitat destruction, plummeted to near-extinction by the 1900s. It was restored to ample "harvesting" levels only by conservationist work in midcentury.

Developing at the same time as this indiscriminate field shooting was the more organized turkey shoot for prizes. In the typical nineteenth-century shoot, or match, captive turkeys were placed in a pen surrounded by a wooden shield at approximately chest level. The targets were the birds' bobbing heads, and the marksman's prize was the body of the turkey that he had decapitated with his shot. The notion that good sports always aim for the head survives in turkey hunter etiquette today.

The final development in the turkey shoot was the substitution, in this century, of paper targets for the bobbing heads. As rural turkey shoots are now run, the marksman with the highest score against these targets brings home a (usually frozen) turkey prize. It's a far more rationalized system of proving prowess than picking them off out of the trees, and it shows how completely marketing prerogatives have taken over entertainment and food delivery alike.

RED FOR HUNTING

In societies in which hunting is a matter of survival, the task is accomplished by solitary hunters or small bands, none of whom would ever don red clothing before going into the woods. In our society, red is a necessary (and generally legally required) protection for two reasons. First is the amateur status of most hunters, coupled with, or rather abetted by, the easy availability of guns in our culture. Wearing bright clothing may diminish one's chances of sneaking up on a deer, but it has the considerable compensation of protecting ill-trained marksmen from each other. This is not a necessity in traditional societies, where hunting, far from being merely an escapist pastime, is an essential way of making a living.

The second reason that a warning color must be worn is the congestion of our hunting areas. A hundred years ago, the American hunter might have been as isolated in the bush as the African. But as overhunting and the destruction of game habitats severely depleted the size of available forest "harvests," state and local conservation forces had to restrict hunting in both range and duration. This resulted in today's posted areas, both public and private, where even red-capped bravos may not venture; hence, too, the prohibition against killing does, the individual hunters' bag limit, and, most important, the extremely narrow window of opportunity that hunters are afforded in the calendar. Because open season on most game is so short, that season and the opening day in particular finds the population density of hunters rivaling that of the hunted. In such a congested arena, it would be irrational not to sacrifice stealth for the sake of self-protection.

MAPLE SUGARING

The English colonists, who did not utilize the sap of their homeland's maple trees, learned maple sugaring from the American Indians. They took to it quickly because, as John Mariani points out, maple sugar was cheaper than West Indian cane sugar. In the nineteenth century, maple-bred sugars and syrups continued to compete favorably with cane products, which suffered not only from import duties but also from the enmity of abolitionists: Mariani quotes one who urged Americans to refuse Caribbean sugar in order to "reduce by that much the lashings the Negroes have to endure to grow cane sugar to satisfy our gluttony." Thus finances and morality combined to make maple products "principal forms of sweetening" for Americans well into the century.

In New England, particularly, where the weather was most conducive to sugaring, every family with sap trees on its property would each spring tap out the sugar bush, or woods in which sugar maples predominate. Families with large sugar bushes were able to supplement their other income by producing sugar and syrups for profit. Such family-based sugaring-off operations are still common throughout New England, and their nostalgic value as a traditional backcountry custom is attested to by the fact that thousands of tourists scour Vermont every March to watch the sap boiling and to buy.

EATING CONTESTS

The eating contest, as practiced at state fairs and ethnic festivals around the country, typifies two fundamental traits in the American character: the appreciation of natural abundance and the competitive drive to consume. The standard "stuff yer face" affair is an amalgam of slapstick and determined excess, a kind of enshrinement of gorging that could have been perfected only in a culture with a copious range of regional delicacies and faith in the axiom that more is better. Americans have always been devotees of the "groaning board" approach to cuisine, and if grease on the chin whiskers and meringue in the eyebrows lend a parodistic flavor to the proceedings, still the classic kielbasa-gobbling or pie-eating contest is essentially a mere extension of the national eating style in general. It mimics the American mania for conspicuous consumption.

BINGO

Bingo is clearly a form of gambling. Technically, since players buy a chance to win, it is a lottery, but since the game can provide a reasonably sure income for organizations with a relatively low risk for the players, church and civic groups have often encouraged it, even though wagering is, strictly speaking, a "vice." The logic seems to be utilitarian: The stakes are low enough (usually a dollar a card) to prevent serious financial injury, and the softening of morals that gambling entails is a necessary evil to be condoned so that the church heating bill may be paid.

There may also be a social justification. In an article on the demographics of bingo players, Laura Delind notes that the majority of them are older, lower-middle-class women who lack both the financial resources and the social networks to engage in a wide range of activities. "Their commonality," she says, "seemed to be their possession of considerable leisure time, a bit of excess capital and a certain social or personal isolation—as expressed in relationships which were typically of one dimension and devoid of choice." That's a good thumbnail sketch of the position of many seniors in this culture, and it may provide a secondary reason that churches so often sponsor the game. Encouraging aging community members to maintain social contacts with each other, even in a "vice-ridden" atmosphere, may be construed as pastoral concern.

MATCHES AT CONCERTS

One of the arresting moments at any well-received rock performance is the lighting of matches by the audience in farewell homage to the musicians. Grateful Dead fans claim with absolute conviction that this charming custom was invented by an appreciative Deadhead audience sometime in the late 1960s. Fans of Bruce Springsteen and Bob Dylan claim the same thing, with as much conviction, and it would be next to impossible to determine where the practice first started. What is interesting is that, in the age of spectacular special effects and monstrous walls of sound, rock audiences should have chosen such a small, quiet method of paying tribute. It's as if they are attempting to recapture some of the ancestral magic of ceremonial song—to evoke the flickering calm of the prerock era, when music and magic had not diverged, and when the light of candles or bonfires was a natural accompaniment to musical performance. This unconscious evocation of an ancestral, preelectronic past is entirely appropriate to the rock medium, since rock concerts have now taken the place of communal sacrifices, and performers have become our high priests.

PAPERING A HOUSE

One of the more egregious pieces of mischief engaged in by adolescent vandals is the "papering" of houses and surrounding trees. This practice involves hurling rolls of toilet paper skyward, so that it lands in limp festoons, like scatological spaghetti. Fraternity boys are fond of thus decorating the houses of their rivals, and it might be supposed that in these cases the message being conveyed is purely, and competitively, insulting. Adorning someone's residence with toilet paper is a symbolic way of defecating on his property. Yet the adornment is festive as well (at least until the rain comes), resembling not so much an unmentionable household item as wayward streamers from a giant's parade. So there may be a good-natured, even friendly, aspect to the custom: In a curiously inverted manner, it hints at intimacy.

SPELLING BEES

The spelling bee is a peculiarly American institution, and the model for this orthographic competition was proposed by the nation's first great champion of self-improvement, Benjamin Franklin. In his interesting survey of the custom, Allen Walker Read (1941) cited Franklin's pedagogical advice that excellence in spelling be encouraged by "pairing the scholars" in a classroom and having each attempt to stump the other. Late-eighteenth-century schoolrooms adopted this method widely, and by the early years of the nineteenth century, these "trials in spelling" had moved out of the schools into the community. Spelling contests had become so popular that they had to be held after school hours, with parents and friends, not just teachers, observing the proceedings. These well-attended events became known as bees, and they were as important as quilting bees or corn-husking bees in providing entertainment and social union in rural communities. As Read notes, they also provided a "conservative," or regularizing, influence on American speech, a kind of populist imprimatur to the standardization that Noah Webster had urged in his dictionaries.

The spelling bee fell out of favor in the East around the middle of the century, but it retained its appeal on the culture-hungry frontier until well into the 1900s. Radio picked it up in the 1930s, and even television adopted the form in the 1950s. One of the bona-fide highlights of the eventually discredited quiz show "The $64,000 Question" was the successful spelling by a black schoolgirl of the word *antidisestablishmentarianism.*

CHAIN LETTERS

The chain letter, in Alan Dundes's apt phrase, is a "folk geometric progression" in which riches, happiness, or other rewards are supposed to accrue to the participants as the result of a trivial investment. The typical letter includes a statement proclaiming that the letter is a chain letter, an injunction to send copies to friends, usually within a set period of time, a description of the benefits that will follow, and a warning of what might happen if the instructions are ignored, that is, if the reader "breaks the chain." Probably every teenager in America has received such a letter at least once, but the practice is not confined to the young or to this country. The French have their *chaîne de bonheur,* or "chain of happiness," and the Germans their *Briefe zum Himmel,* or "letters to heaven."

Dundes gives two intelligent readings of the custom. In a 1966 article, citing a "joke" letter in which the reward is sexual partners and an "academic" letter in which it is advertisement of one's own publications, he suggests that the chain letter is a "socially sanctioned outlet or excuse for the overt expression of an actual wish." This interpretation applies just as well to the most common form of such letters, those that promise overnight wealth. The chain form, with its tandem promise and warning, obliges the reader to participate in a process that is attractive to him anyway. As Dundes says, "Clearly the fact that folklore so often 'obliges' us to do what we really want to do is one reason why there will always be folklore."

In a subsequent analysis (1975), Dundes links this obligatory process to two of our most enduring cultural values: conformity to norms and the dream of wealth. Chain letters reward the gray-flannel mind, the people who, accepting what they have been told, go along with the system to achieve success. "In the case of a financial investment," Dundes writes, "one is asked to invest a modest amount in the hope of multiplying one's investment, surely the guiding principle of capitalism." Thus the chain letter provides food for the myth that, in America, anyone can make it.

Is it because the government realizes this myth has already been oversold that the Post Office makes chain letters illegal? Officially they are banned under the fraud laws, but since virtually all chain letters include the proviso "If no one breaks the chain," it is hard to see how fraud is involved. One might just as logically jail a stockbroker who promises you a good return on an investment "assuming current market trends continue."

SINGING TELEGRAMS

The first singing telegram was offered by the Postal Telegraph Company in 1933 as a way of boosting flagging business during the Depression. It has continued to be a popular novelty greeting in this century probably because it introduces a homey note into a form of communication that, from its inception, had tended toward the coldly formal. The excitement of receiving a telegram in the nineteenth century must always have been tempered with some uneasiness, not only because telegrams frequently brought bad news, but also because their relative high cost, the so-much-per-word limitation, tended to make telegram messages more formulaic and abrupt than a personal letter would have been. The introduction of the telephone made the telegram seem all the more distant. The singing variety has remained a colorful option, most likely because it repersonalizes an inherently depersonalized format.

PERSONAL-ADVICE COLUMNS

Everybody needs advice, and everybody is nosy. These two "universal facts about human nature," Clark Hendley suggests, explain the
overwhelming popularity of advice columns—especially the Miss
Lonelyhearts variety, in which the problems posed are frequently
romantic ones. The advice column is neither a universal genre nor
a very old one. The secret of its popularity may be human nature,
but its proximate precursor was the eighteenth-century popular
press—that often vitriolic and always highly opinionated literary
arena in which such luminaries as Joseph Addison, Richard Steele,
and Daniel Defoe made their reputations.

The first example of the genre was John Dunton's London peri-
odical *The Athenian Mercury,* a question-and-answer vehicle that
ran from 1691 to the end of the century and that served as the
prototype for various eighteenth-century journals, including
Defoe's *Little Review.* Unlike followers of today's advice columns,
Dunton's readers were less interested in affairs of the heart than
they were in religion and the natural sciences. About 20 percent of
the paper's queries asked for scientific information rather than advice, on such topics as the eating habits of birds and the buoyancy
of rain clouds. So many people had questions about religion that
Dunton enlisted the Rev. Samuel Wesley (father of John Wesley)
to field them. (One question that fascinated readers well into the
eighteenth century was the identity of Cain's wife. That one is still
up for grabs.)

The current interest in personal questions would seem to be a
break with this tradition, but in a curious way it's an outgrowth. The
seventeenth century was a watershed between the late medieval
world and the more atomized and secular world of today. In a sense
the very fact that theology and science were being discussed in public
forums at that time indicated a shift in sensibility toward the personal and away from ecclesiastical hegemony. Nathaniel West, author of the classic American novel *Miss Lonelyhearts,* exaggerated
only a little when he called the modern heirs of Dunton and Defoe
"the priests of twentieth-century America." Hendley, I think, has it
right: The secularism of our time, with all its emphasis on *individual*
problems, began in the seventeenth century, "when the traditional
roles of advisor and confessor were taken from the church and

transplanted to that most secular of modern institutions, the newspaper." In his nice phrase, we now have Dear Abby as Mother Confessor.

WRITING ON BATHROOM WALLS

The practice of scratching invitations, boasts, and obscenities on bathroom walls is at least 2,000 years old and seems to have changed little in that time. The excavated walls of ancient Pompeii, buried by Vesuvian ash in A.D. 79, display such gems of the scribbler's art as "Hic ego puellas multas futui" (Here I fucked many girls) and "Si qui futuere volet Atticen quaerat a XVI" (If you want to fuck, call Attica at No. 16). In his pioneering study of North American graffiti, Allen Walker Read (1935), noting the similarity between these and modern examples, joked that Americans were "merely carrying on the classical tradition."

In Peoria no less than in Pompeii, the most striking features of that tradition have always been male braggadocio and the adolescent desire to embarrass. Folklorist Alan Dundes, in an article entitled "Here I Sit," explains why. Following psychoanalyst Ernest Jones's description of "anal-erotic character traits," he suggests that defacing latrine walls may reflect a "primitive smearing impulse," that is, the infantile desire to manipulate and advertise one's feces. Drawing a link between feces-production and writing, Dundes cites one of the most common bathroom ditties, the scatological quatrain that begins "Those who write on shithouse walls / Roll their shit in little balls," and concludes that the point of bathroom writing is to place symbolic "dirt" in public view.

BAR CONVERSATIONS

Conversational etiquette in a bar is in a sense the opposite of that in an elevator. Bars are what Erving Goffman (1963) called "open regions," arenas in which conversation may be offered, without giving offense, to anyone present, and with the expectation of response. Obviously the openness of bars varies, but I think that Sherri Cavan is right in saying that the door to a bar is a symbolic entrance to sociability, and that those who enter declare simply by doing so (unless they announce otherwise—for example, by hunkering into a corner) that they are "available for interaction."

But this basic situation has some important corollaries that tend to deflate rather than enhance sociability. Cavan notes that even though the initiation of conversation is "open," its continuance is typically "closed," because bar tête-à-têtes are "subject to a variety of contingencies that make them always tentative and often superficial." Specifically, bar conversations between strangers must stay within the confines of small talk, may be terminated abruptly by either party, and may be discounted, or "ignored," by either party once they have run their course. (In this last sense particularly, bar conversations are like liquor-fueled chitchat in general; they are interactions about which one can, either honestly or conveniently, say "I don't remember saying that.")

Because of their tentative, evanescent nature, Cavan labels bar conversation as "time out" behavior. These encounters are psychologically necessary excursions from the "serious" business of daily life. They are not to be taken seriously, so the range of permissible language, especially sexual language, is often extended beyond the norm even within the context of small talk.

BUYING SOMEONE A DRINK

Tavern etiquette generally requires that you engage a person in light conversation for a few minutes before offering to buy him or her a drink, although in bars where mixing and matching are obviously the main order of business, it is permissible to initiate the conversation with the opening line, "What are you drinking?" In both cases, the proffered drink serves the same purpose: It registers the buyer's interest in social discourse and invites the other party to respond.

The manner of response, however, is strictly defined by rules of gender and sexual inclination. In the vast majority of cases, it is a man who offers the first drink. When the recipient is another man, he is expected to return the favor as the conversation proceeds—if he wishes the conversation to proceed. (If he is uninterested in the conversation, of course, or if he is in a hurry to leave the bar, he may promise to "get you next time" or simply refuse the drink in the first place.) When the recipient is a woman, however, as Sherri Cavan acutely points out, the offer to return a purchased drink decodes as a rebuff. It is more likely to terminate than to prolong the conversation. The reason for this, it would seem, is that buying a drink for a strange woman, in a culture that demands male control, is a kind of down payment for sexual favors. It is the first installment of an "investment" plan in which the next, larger installment would be a dinner. If a woman "pays back" the favor, it is her way of saying she is uninterested, or in transactional terms, "We're even. Now I don't owe you anything."

This neat structure, of course, has been considerably complicated by the rise of the women's and gay rights movements. With the increase in female vice-presidents and with the uncloseting of homosexuals of both genders, it is now more difficult to determine, in a given social situation, who owes whom what when a drink is bought. The rules of thumb I have just described probably exist in pure form only in heterosexual singles bars.

DANCE PARTNERS

In our society women may dance with women, but men may not dance with men. There is more to this prohibition, I think, than the often-noted abhorrence that American males have for the idea that they may have homosexual tendencies. In prohibiting male contact through dancing, folk custom reinforces a fundamental precept about gender: the social-Darwinist notion that real men are competitive and naturally fight with each other for social eminence. Dancing, by its nature, requires cooperation, a virtue on which few American men set a high value. That is why they don't—indeed, can't—dance with each other.

The primacy of competition over cooperation also explains why it is the man who must lead. Women are conditioned in two directions. They are taught to lead (that is, to be good, strong mothers), and they are taught to follow (that is, to be good, obedient wives). This dual training is what makes them able dancers, whether their partners are women or men. Men are taught *only* to lead, which is what dooms them to unresponsiveness. Men lead on the dance floor for the same reason that they lead in politics. It's not because they are inherently better at it than women, but because, having been raised on patriarchal principles, it is the only step they know.

DRIVE-IN MOVIES

The American drive-in movie had its golden age at the same time as the drive-in restaurant, in the decade immediately following World War II, when among the leading indicators of postwar affluence were the classic gas-eaters of the 1950s and the two-car garage. But the drive-in also tied in neatly to two other sociocultural developments of that time. First was the coming of age of the baby boomers. The original drive-in movie operators understood better than any sociologists that the car and its teenager cannot be parted, and in spite of advertisements aimed (often successfully) at attracting the family market, a principal source of drive-in income in those years was the carload (or carloads) of teenagers; the dominance of that market was evident in the prevalence of sci-fi and teen romance movies. Second was television. The expansion into drive-ins was a desperate move on the part of a decaying studio system to recapture some of the attention lost to the new medium, and in this effort Hollywood was mildly successful. Between 1948 and 1956, the number of movie theaters in the United States was cut in half, but approximately four thousand new drive-ins helped to make up for the loss. Today many of those units have closed, but the drive-in remains an American artifact. In rural parts of the country, it retains its folkloric hold on succeeding generations of teenagers.

DEMOLITION DERBIES

A demolition derby is a large-scale bumping-car rodeo. Entrants pay a fee to drive dilapidated automobiles into an arena and, at the starting gun, commence driving them into each other, with the last car moving declared the winner. On the surface this display of mechanized mayhem would seem to have no other purpose than to channel the culture's notorious aggressive urge into a socially acceptable form of entertainment. But that purpose is well-served by other activities, such as football and boxing, and I would suggest that there is an additional appeal to the demo derby that those sports do not provide. It might be called, to twist a phrase from Thorstein Veblen, the appeal of conspicuous destruction.

In a classic ethnography of Kwakiutl Indian life, Ruth Benedict described what she called "a parody of our own economic arrangements": a property-destruction ceremony in which the highest social status accrued to the village leader who burned the greatest number of his possessions. Might we see in the auto demolition "ceremony" an updated and somewhat rationalized version of this scenario? The Kwakiutl typically burned blankets, candlefish oil, and, in some cases, their houses; these items were chosen not because they were dispensable, but precisely because they were valuable. Since there are very few items in contemporary American culture more highly valued than the automobile, we might see the destruction of such possessions as a parody on the parody.

CITIZENS BAND RADIO

The Federal Communications Commission first made radio channel space available for public use in 1958, and for fifteen years the number of applications for licenses was minimal. Then, in 1973, as the oil crunch got under way, the CB phenomenon took off, as first truckers and then nonprofessional drivers adopted the new technology as a means of battling the hated 55-mile-per-hour speed limit. Americans are a cussedly independent breed, and in spite of widespread evidence that the speed reduction was saving both lives and gasoline, many drivers were unwilling to let the politicians dictate how fast they should tear up the highways. So CB radio quickly became a populist weapon, enabling drivers to alert each other not only to the availability of low fuel prices, but also to the whereabouts of radar traps.

The very fact that Americans should band together in violation of the law suggests, perhaps, unfulfilled revolutionary tendencies on the part of a frequently complacent populace. It harks back to a romanticized outlaw tradition that has always seen Billy the Kid as a more interesting character than Wyatt Earp. One interesting aspect of this tradition, as updated by the eighteen-wheelers, is analyzed well by

Richard David Ramsey. In the ongoing battle between "the people" and "Smokey the Bear," he notes, the CBers' argot plays a crucial role, because like racial argot it tends simultaneously to create group identity and to confound outsiders. To announce over the band that you are "putting the hammer down" acknowledges to your accomplices that you are about to break the "double nickle" limit, but in a language that the enemy, theoretically, cannot understand. To state "This is that Piccolo Pete, good buddy" is to reinforce the exclusivity of what Ramsey calls the "clandestine nationwide society—a secret organization in which the members go by handles or nicknames." Like underworld and ghetto slang, therefore, CB jargon does more than communicate facts. It "exemplifies self-defense, hostility, and desire to preserve identity and solidarity."

HITCHHIKING

Hitchhiking arose in the 1930s, when people "hit the road" more often from necessity than for pleasure. The original hitchers were the hoboes of that era, and the term first appeared in their milieu. It spread through the armed forces in the 1940s and 1950s, and in the 1960s was transformed into a kind of national mania by members of the hippie subculture. If this particular type of ride-begging has become less common in the yuppy era, that fact has as much to do with safety as with finances. The publicity given to crimes of the road has made it seem chancier than it used to be to get from New York to Oklahoma on a dime.

As for the specifics of the custom, Harold Wentworth and Stuart Berg Flexner claim that "the universally accepted method" is to face the oncoming traffic and "to raise one's right arm, elbow bent, with the hand closed into a fist and the thumb extended in the direction one wishes to travel." A good description of the *American* method. In many parts of Europe, you solicit a ride by walking on the same side of the road and in the same direction as the car traffic, and extend the thumb of your roadside arm toward the front. Your back is to the oncoming traffic in this position, which is a disadvantage in terms of safety, but your progress is not impeded by walking backward. The message of the European method is, "I'm going your way. Help me if you want. I really don't care." The American method seems to announce, "I'm looking straight at you, and I want your help. I'm not afraid if you're not." Americans seem to take, in other words, a more challenging, but also a more optimistic, approach to the situation.

PILGRIMAGE TO MICKEY

Devout Jews visit the Wailing Wall in Jerusalem; devout Catholics visit Lourdes; devout Muslims try to get to Mecca at least once before they die; and devout and not-so-devout Americans go to Disneyland. That is the provocative conjecture of Conrad Kottak (1982), who sees Disneyland and Walt Disney World as not just elaborate amusement parks but national "shrines." Like the holy city of Islam, he notes, each Disney park has both an outer, secular domain—the host city—and an inner, sacred domain, appropriately called the Magic Kingdom. When the "pilgrim" approaches the Magic Kingdom, he parks his car in a huge lot presided over by tutelary "giants" represented by "totemlike" designations: Minnie, Pluto, Goofy, and so on. The visitor is advised to memorize the name of his or her personal guardian ("Minnie, Minnie, Minnie") so that he can remember where he has parked. Passing into the park itself is like going through a typical "passage rite," in which you leave your mundane, secular identity behind, divest yourself of certain worldly goods (the admission price), and enter a new reality. This new reality is both futuristic (Tomorrowland) and nostalgic (Main Street, U.S.A.). In a sense it transcends time, like a religious experience. At the same time, the Disney experience reinforces beliefs of the national secular religion. In the Hall of Presidents, particularly, the American pilgrim is reminded of the noble deeds of his ancestors and is enjoined to live up to their examples. Finally, when the pilgrim leaves the shrine, he is strongly encouraged to bring away sacred relics (souvenirs) that both embody and remind him of the experience. Kottak's specific analogies may seem whimsical, but the fundamental linkage is surely not. He is right on target when he says that the Disney experience constitutes "a powerful complex of enculturative forces in contemporary American society."

SMOKING

In one of his early monologues, comedian Bob Newhart played Walter Raleigh's London-based agent, explaining hilariously in PR jargon why the adventurer's latest discovery, tobacco, would never catch on in England: "Let me get this straight, Walt. You roll leaves up in paper, set fire to 'em, and suck the smoke into your lungs?" Phrased like that, the custom sounds ridiculous, but it did catch on and has been going strong ever since, in spite of the Surgeon General's warnings. One basic reason for smoking's popularity, Michael Starr has shown, is that, in the United States at least, it has always been promoted as a highly masculine practice. The obvious phallic imagery aside, the dangling cigarette has been used, since around the time of World War I, as an iconographic emblem of The Male. It was only after World War II that the female market was seriously tapped, and interestingly, the first "women's cigarette," the "sissified," filter-tipped Marlboro, was soon transformed by ad agencies into the ultimate symbol of American virility. In a reverse irony, it was a "cool," silently macho style of cigarette, Silva Thins, that ultimately led to the "modern woman's" favorite, the supposedly feminist Virginia Slims.

The original association of the cigarette with a Bogart-type masculinity has broken down in recent years, as more and more women pick up the habit and as the tobacco companies milk that lucrative market. But the reason that people begin smoking in the first place has probably not changed much over the years. New smokers are recruited from the young teenagers eager to adopt the habit that movies and advertisements continue to claim as the mark of a real man or at least an adult. Conveniently for the cigarette companies, teenagers are still ignorant enough to take this equation at face value. After they have smoked for a couple of years, nicotine dependency takes over, and by that time "brand loyalty" is established.

PASSING THE JOINT

Marijuana etiquette, since at least the heyday of the 1960s counter-culture, has stipulated that whenever the drug is consumed among friends, it be passed from one person to another freely, until all who wish to smoke have had the opportunity to do so. Like the North American Indian pipe-passing from which it distantly derives, joint-passing among modern dope smokers symbolically pacifies and unites the circle of participants. Whatever the ultimate effect of the drug itself on the atmosphere, its initial meaning is one of communion. In this sense, it is precisely opposed to the individualistic iconography of tobacco smoking. The archetypal tobacco-smoker in popular culture is still probably Humphrey Bogart, whose lone-wolf image was enhanced by his frequent attribute, the personal cigarette. No dope smoker, in company, can have a personal cigarette, and it is therefore entirely appropriate that to hold on to a joint too long without passing it is contemptuously known as "Bogarting."

RED-LETTER DAYS:

HOLIDAYS

NEW YEAR'S EVE

Why do we go crazy on New Year's Eve? Why the exotic costumes, the masked balls, the noisemakers, the excessive drinking, the general air of orgiastic frenzy that makes the last day of the year so distinctive? The great historian of religion Mircea Eliade claimed that the New Year's celebrations of many primitive peoples were an attempt to begin history anew out of the chaos of the primordial "time before time." The activities with which we moderns welcome the New Year are remarkably similar to activities that traditional peoples used to reconstruct order out of that chaos. They wore masks to represent the spirits of the dead, who would have to be incorporated into the reborn year. They beat drums and shouted and raised a general hue and cry as a way of scaring off demons. They indulged themselves in alcoholic and sexual excess as a way of evoking the chaos that would soon be banished. They took the fights that often grew out of this indulgence as ceremonial battles between the old year and the new, a rationale that our street brawlers have forgotten. We may even see, in these primitive rites, a prefiguring of our New Year's resolutions, for the "purgations, purifications, and confessing of sins" that often characterized ancient end-of-the-year festivals are conceptually very similar. All in all, the inspired madness of the contemporary New Year's Eve reflects precisely the hope of the primitive: the hope that tomorrow will be different.

"AULD LANG SYNE"

The custom of singing "Auld Lang Syne" at midnight on New Year's Eve is the remnant of a broader custom of ending all parties with the song, often with the participants joining hands in a circle. This larger custom originated in the British Isles around the end of the eighteenth century. It was particularly (and originally) popular in Scotland, because the plaintive lyrics of the song were written in 1788 by Scotland's national folk poet, Robert Burns; the Burns version was first printed in the song collection *Scots Musical Museum,* published in 1796, the year of his death.

I say Burns version because there were others. British opera composer William Shield used the melody in his 1783 work *Rosina.* It has also been attributed to the seventeenth-century writer Francis Sempill, and to one of the first Scots writers to use English, Shakespeare's contemporary Sir Robert Aytoun. The musicological consensus is that the tune was a traditional Scottish folk melody, and that these writers, Robbie Burns included, tinkered only with the words, not the song. Burns himself claimed that he took down the basics from "an old man's singing," and that it was an "old song of the olden times." It was an apt description, given that "auld lang syne" in the Scots dialect means "old long since," or (roughly) the good old days.

THE GROUNDHOG'S SHADOW

February 2 is the date that Europeans know as Candlemas Day, celebrating the purification of the Virgin Mary after her delivery of the infant Jesus. For reasons that are obscure, the weather on this late-winter day was traditionally thought to be a kind of reverse indicator of what was to come: Fine weather indicated a prolonged winter, while clouds and chill presaged an early spring. From the Middle Ages on, country folk believed that on this day hibernating animals left their dens to inspect the state of the sky. It was believed of bears, badgers, and particularly hedgehogs that if they saw their shadows on that day, planting should be delayed for several weeks. The American Groundhog Day is a transformation of this custom, with the North American groundhog, or woodchuck, taking the place of the Old World hedgehog. This is an interesting transformation, since the hedgehog is a spiny little creature that is not very closely related, in appearance, to the woodchuck. If the German settlers who brought the tradition to America had paid more attention to physical resemblance, we might now celebrate Porcupine Day.

VALENTINES

Valentine's Day is named for two early Christian martyrs, neither of them a champion of romantic love. Their common feast day was February 14, which became known as a lover's holiday because of two historical coincidences: The ancient Roman festival of the Lupercalia, frequently marked by licentiousness, was celebrated on February 15, and a medieval folk tradition maintained that the springtime mating of birds took place on St. Valentine's Day. This latter belief led, by the fourteenth century, to the custom of choosing by lot a valentine, or sweetheart for a day. Messages of affection passed between these randomly chosen lovers were precursors of the modern valentine card.

Credit for writing the first valentine verses is often given to Charles, Duke of Orleans, who as a prisoner of war in 1415 sent his wife romantic poems from an English cell. But this seems more a unique incident than the fount of a tradition. In tracing the development of the printed valentine, Frank Staff mentions the seventeenth-century custom of presenting one's lot-chosen valentine with love tokens or "prettily written letters," but he assures us that the first real valentines per se—that is, greeting cards specially made for the holiday—did not appear until the eighteenth century. By the 1780s printed cards were becoming common, especially in Germany, where they were called *Freundschaftkarten,* or "friendship cards." In England handwritten valentines were still common toward the close of the century, although standardization was already setting in. Staff notes a typical contemporary handbook called *The Complete British Valentine Writer, or the High Road to Love for Both Sexes,* which gave literary advice and examples for amateur writers.

THE HEART SHAPE

The *Oxford English Dictionary* says that the heart was considered "the seat of love and affection" as early as the twelfth century, so it is not surprising to find so-called heart shapes appearing on valentines. But you don't need to be a cardiologist to realize that the conventionalized heart shape—the symmetrical, double-lobed figure that tapers to a point at the bottom—looks about as much like a real heart as a pentangle looks like a star. What it does look like, Desmond Morris (1985) speculates, is a stylized human buttocks—the anatomical area that nonhuman primates all recognize as sexually stimulating, and that might well have triggered, in the amorous subconscious of some early doodler of heart shapes, the current, conventional design. Taking this observation as a start, we might also say that the valentine shape suggests a female torso with prominent breasts and the once-fashionable "wasp waist," as well as the imprint that might remain on a paper kissed by milady's ruby lips.

WASHINGTON'S BIRTHDAY SALES

The birthday of the United States' first national hero was celebrated publicly beginning in the 1780s and became an annual occasion during his presidency (1789–1796). Throughout those years, the date was Washington's actual birthday, February 11. It was shifted to the current date, February 22, in 1796, to follow the "corrected" New Style calendar that had been established in 1752. But even after the General's death in 1800 led to a national day of mourning on February 22, celebrations of his birthday remained irregular until the centennial of his birth in 1832. From then until just after the Civil War, when Lincoln-worship began to take precedence, Washington was widely revered as something akin to a saint, not only on his birthday but throughout the year.

Today the patriotic oratory of those years has been replaced by more mercantile celebrations, as store owners increasingly transform the date into an opportunity to empty their shelves of excess midwinter stock. In advertising for these events, they take as much advantage as possible of the three most enduring legends of Washington's life: the cherry tree story ("We chop our prices for you"), the silver dollar across the Potomac story ("Silver Dollar Sale"), and the "cannot tell a lie" tag (especially useful in combined Truthful George–Honest Abe promotions). The irony is that all of these stories are lies. They were invented in 1800 by Mason Locke Weems, an itinerant preacher and bookseller who singlehandedly created the spotless Washington in his biography of that year. Historian Daniel Boorstin has called this book "perhaps the most widely read, most influential book ever written about American history."

LEAP-YEAR PROPOSALS

For several centuries, European folk custom has said that a woman may propose marriage in leap year. According to a London pamphlet of 1606, the custom was "part of the common lawe in regard to the social relations of life." If a man should refuse the lady's offer, custom further stipulated, he must present her a consolation prize of a silk gown.

The idea of setting aside one year in four for female initiative is, George Stimpson (1948) says, "of considerable antiquity," although no date earlier than 1606 has been found. Antiquarians have stated that a thirteenth-century Scottish parliament made the custom a law, but history books do not confirm the legend. Equally legendary is the idea that the custom originated with St. Patrick, in the days before clerics were barred from marriage. The abbess St. Bridget, goes the tale, complained to Patrick on behalf of her fellow nuns that they could not pop the question to their admirers. Equity in the matter being inconceivable, the two saints arrived at a compromise whereby each fourth year the sisters would be given the prerogative. Patrick, vowed to celibacy, had to give Bridget the gown, rather than himself.

Legend though the story may be, it does have a heuristic value, in that it hints at a source of social tension, the enforced passivity of females, and responds in a manner that favors the status quo. With only one-quarter of the time being surrendered, and with even that concession qualified by the silk gown rider, the situation reflects a maintaining of male control, while seeming to rebuke it. So female initiative has remained, like the one-day reversal of the slave-master relationship in ancient Rome, a temporary and jocular expedient.

ST. PATRICK'S DAY PARADE

There are now St. Patrick's Day parades in many cities with large Irish populations, but the largest, and the model, is still New York's. This event, now a predictable part of March 17 television programming, began in 1763, when small groups of Irish followed the cobblestones to celebratory feasts at their local taverns. After the American Revolution, such informal marches became a little more organized, when a veterans group called the Friendly Sons of Saint Patrick began advertising both their patriotism and their ancestry in yearly walks. Joe McCarthy notes that these events were often bitterly resented by onlookers of British ancestry, with St. Patrick frequently hung in effigy to taunt the shamrock-loving vets. Ensuing brawls often became so violent that, in 1803, New York banned such effigies, under pain of a ten-dollar fine.

With the influx of poor Catholic Irish to New York following the potato famine of the 1840s, religious and political tensions increased, and throughout the first half of the century, the annual parades often provoked violence. As early as 1838, to defend themselves, Irish Catholics delegated the management of the marches to the protective Ancient Order of the Hibernians. It was this organization, McCarthy says, that converted the parade "from a rough and informal social outing to a large, well-organized civil rights demonstration." In 1844 this group had to defend the old St. Patrick's Cathedral, in lower Manhattan, against an anti-Catholic mob.

With the growing power of Irish militias and the growing influence of the Irish in New York politics, the parade gradually quieted down. By 1879, when the new cathedral on Fifth Avenue was dedicated, the civil rights aspect of the march had become muted. Today it has been all but forgotten, with, as the tipsy might have it, "everybody feeling Irish for a day."

DRINKING ON ST. PATRICK'S DAY

The consumption of green beer, or any other drink, on St. Patrick's Day is less a separate holiday custom than an extension of Irish drinking in general. Despite the fact that the Irish are only moderately heavy drinkers by European standards (the Belgians and Germans both consume more beer), the image of the Irish drunk remains a popular one in America, partly because of successful stereotyping by Irish-baiting Americans in the nineteenth century and partly because, in Irish culture, drink has long been applauded as much as abhorred. Why? According to Peter Farb and George Armelagos, because Ireland has always been a poor, famine-torn country, and alcohol has long served there as an intermittent substitute for food. It has provided the "social and psychological satisfaction, as well as the caloric energy" that other people get from heavier diets; in addition, strong drink—especially the traditional cottage dweller's *poteen*—has long been credited with medicinal value, as a prophylactic against the damp climate. Hence the medically inaccurate folk belief that a shot of whisky can "warm a body up," and the Guinness Company's long-standing advertising claim "Guinness is good for you."

Once alcohol began to serve as an occasional food substitute, necessity was turned into a virtue, and the "socializing" advantages were emphasized. By the time of the great Irish migrations to America in the nineteenth century, the link between liquor and conviviality had already been forged, and "strong drink became synonymous with hospitality."

SHAMROCKS

Shamrock means "little clover" in Gaelic, and the plant's popularity as an emblem of Ireland can be traced to a legend about St. Patrick, the fifth-century British-born monk who converted the Irish to Christianity. The Emerald Islanders at that time were given to piracy and brigandage. They had captured the future saint as a teenager and sold him into slavery. His later missionary calling to the island was a way of paying back this rude folk with kindness. The difficulty of his task was aggravated by a lack of rational subtlety on the part of the pagan Irish, in particular their inability to understand the Christian doctrine of the Trinity. To get across the message that the god he served was three persons in one, Patrick is said to have used the shamrock as a visual aid. Its trefoil form perfectly illustrated the mystery.

MARDI GRAS

It is not accidental that Mardi Gras, the springtime frenzy that New Orleans imported from France, should so closely resemble New Year's Eve, for in ancient times the new year commonly began in the spring, and was welcomed by orgiastic celebration. The wildness of Carnival, no less than that of New Year's Eve, evokes primitive rites of renewal. But there is a more immediate background to the New Orleans celebrations, reflected in the festival's two common names. *Carnival,* from the Latin, means "farewell to meat," and *Mardi Gras,* which is French, means literally "Fat Tuesday." Both terms refer to the period of festivity and banqueting that preceded Lent in the medieval church calendar. In the early Middle Ages this period often began as early as Epiphany (January 6), so that the original carnivals frequently lasted for as long as Lent itself. Eventually the period was shortened, and today the carnival season is usually about ten days long. The last of those ten days is Fat Tuesday itself, the last chance for the pious to consume meat before the forty-day fast preceding Easter.

ASH WEDNESDAY ASHES

In the Catholic calendar, the first day of Lent is called Ash Wednesday, or the "day of ashes" (in Latin, *dies cinerum*). On that day the faithful receive smudges of ash on their foreheads, as an emblem of their mortality. The administering priest reminds them of the custom's meaning with the formula "Dust thou art, and to dust thou shalt return." The practice, which reflects the Old Testament tradition of wearing sackcloth and ashes as signs of penitence, became Christianized early in Church history—Robert Myers suggests it was during the papacy of Gregory the Great (590–604). Originally the ashes were received only by public penitents. These people had to appear barefooted and in penitential garb at the church door, where the ashes and individual penances would be distributed. As the groups grew in size over time, priests began to adopt the pragmatic course of assuming that everyone was penitent and of distributing ashes to the whole congregation. Thus the rite assumed its current form.

HOT CROSS BUNS

Throughout the British Isles and parts of America, it is customary on Good Friday to eat sweet rolls with an icing cross on the top, as a memento of Christ's passion. With ingenious but tortuous etymology, William Walsh has attempted to link this obviously Christian tradition with the ancient world, by calling the word *bun* a variation of *bous,* the Greek term for a sacred ox, and by seeing the cross as a mutilated "horns of Astarte," the Phoenician goddess of fertility. A far simpler and decidedly traceable explanation is that the custom originated in the medieval abbey of St. Albans, where by the middle of the fourteenth century the monks distributed such rolls to the poor. As Francis Weiser (1954) points out, moreover, the custom of "crossing" one's food, as a blessing and thanks before eating, was widespread in Catholic countries in the Middle Ages. On special occasions the cross was imprinted on bread before baking. Such "precrossed" breads were traditional, especially at Easter and Christmas, in France, Greece, Germany, and the Slavic countries, and the English icing custom is a variant.

APRIL FOOLS

The custom of sending the gullible on fool's errands and of playing other practical jokes on April 1 has been around since at least the Middle Ages and has elicited more than its share of joking explanations. The two most popular ones in the nineteenth century, according to E. Cobham Brewer, were that April was a month of fickle (that is, "fooling") weather, and that the Jews started the custom during

Jesus' passion, by sending him on fool's errands to various magistrates (Annas, Caiaphas, Herod, and finally Pilate) before his crucifixion. An eighteenth-century journalist related the custom to Noah's error of "sending the dove out of the ark before the water had abated" on a date that corresponded to our April 1.

William Walsh rightly ridiculed these speculations and offered a more plausible one. Until 1564, he pointed out, March 25 marked the European New Year, and the festivities associated with its arrival typically lasted eight days, until April 1. With the calendar change of that year, the New Year became January 1, but not everyone immediately got the message. Those who continued to make the New Year's visits and to offer the traditional presents on April 1 would have been accounted April Fools, and eventually these bona fide courtesies were replaced by "pretended gifts and mock ceremonial visits."

That explains why fooling should have become associated with the beginning of April, but, as Walsh himself makes clear, the concept of a day devoted to foolishness is older than the sixteenth century. Both the Roman Saturnalia and the medieval Feast of Fools provided opportunities for the overturning of conventional reason, and indeed the overturning of the social order itself. Slaves were freed at the Saturnalia, and Boy Bishops, Mock Kings, and Lords of Misrule were elected during the Middle Ages. Harvey Cox, in his provocative study of the Feast of Fools, emphasizes its "implicitly radical dimension," and places it within a social context whose flexibility was its capacity for self-mockery. "The divine right of kings, papal infallibility, and the modern totalitarian state," he writes, "all flowered after the Feast of Fools disappeared."

EASTER EGGS

Easter falls officially on the first Sunday after the full moon of March. It is not coincidental that this corresponds with the beginning of spring, for the Christian celebration of Christ's resurrection replicates far more ancient pagan celebrations that have to do with the return of the sun. The deliberate linking of *sun* and *Son* is a motif throughout Christian literature. The name Easter itself, according to

the eighth-century historian the Venerable Bede, derives from Eostre, the Anglo-Saxon dawn goddess. Easter, like Eostre, represents
rebirth: the revival, after darkness, of the soil—or, in Christian
terms, of the soul.

It is because of this association of the holiday with rebirth that
the egg has long been its chief symbol. Alan Watts calls the Easter
egg a modern variant of the ancient World Egg, the symbolic con-
struct that denotes wholeness and that also stands for the "original
germ from which all life proceeds." Francis Weiser (1954) also
mentions the egg as a symbol of spring and of fertility, and notes
that the ancient Persians gave each other eggs at the equinox, just
as Christians do today. In addition, he points out, the egg functioned for Christians as a mundane symbol of Christ's tomb—a
cold and hard casket from which new life ultimately breaks forth in
triumph.

The egg has been a centerpiece of Easter customs for centuries.
American egg-rolling contests, egg hunts, and egg-dyeing all have
their European counterparts. The decoration of eggs is particularly
common, with styles ranging from the pastel monotones that are
most common in the United States to the painstakingly elaborate
filigree work of the Ukraine, which makes its traditional *pysanki*
worthy of display in a museum. In Greece and the Christian Middle
East, eggs are dyed red, probably the original iconographic hue
symbolizing the sacrificial blood of Christ.

THE EASTER BUNNY

The modern Easter bunny is of German origin. Francis Weiser
(1954) cites a sixteenth-century German text in which the animal is
depicted as delivering eggs, and, writing at the end of the nineteenth century, William Walsh said that the "Easter hare" functioned in Germany much like a springtime St. Nicholas: It left colored eggs for good children only. Walsh said that the Easter
connection comes from the animal's association with the moon,
and cited several points of ancient folklore to prove his point. The
hare is nocturnal; the female carries her young for one month; and,
in one of the more curious of the ancients' errors, "both hare and

moon were thought to have the power of changing their sex," since "the new moon was masculine, the waning moon feminine." Easter is "in a sense a lunar holiday" because its date depends on the moon.

These are fascinating but far-fetched speculations. It is more likely that Weiser has it right when he links the bunny to pre-Christian fertility lore: "Hare and rabbit were the most fertile animals our forefathers knew, serving as symbols of abundant new life in the spring season." This speculation has the virtue of explaining the animal's otherwise inexplicable association with eggs.

THE EASTER LILY

Ornamental lilies have been cultivated for about three thousand years, and the family Lilliaceae (which includes the hyancinth, tulip, and garlic) is one of the largest families of flowering plants. The white lily *(Lilium candidum)* has long been associated with Easter, not only because its color traditionally symbolizes purity and joy, but also because two of its morphological features make it a suitable emblem of the resurrection of Christ. Its petals flare out like the bell of a trumpet, suggesting the angel Gabriel's awakening horn. And because it is a bulb it is "buried" and "reborn," thus making it a perfect floral correlate to the death and rebirth of the Savior. In the Middle Ages, incidentally, the lily was associated with the Virgin Mary; hence its common name, Madonna lily.

PASSOVER SEDER

In the Jewish religion, Passover, or Pesach, corresponds to the spring festivals of many ancient religions, but a specific historical basis has made it more durable than most. Passover celebrates the release of the Israelites from bondage, and the term itself refers to the fact that, on the night he slew Egypt's firstborn, God's angel "passed over" the homes of the Jews.

The week-long holiday of Passover commemorates these events chiefly in a meal called the *seder*, or "order," which serves as a family reunion and as a means of transmitting Jewish lore to the younger generation. The meal begins with the chanting of the Exodus story, includes a scriptural question-and-answer sequence initiated by the youngest son, and involves the consumption of traditional foods with symbolic significance. For example, unleavened bread, or *matzoh,* recalls the unrisen bread the Hebrews had to take with them on their hasty departure from Egypt. Bitter herbs stand for the bitterness of bondage. Roasted lamb represents the sacrificial blood that the Hebrews were instructed to smear on their doors as a sign to the angel that they should be spared. And *haroseth,* a mixture of apples, nuts, and wine, represents the clay with which the Jews made bricks for Pharaoh. Wine is also drunk with the meal, and a cup set aside for the prophet Elijah, whose appearance, says tradition, will presage the coming of the Messiah.

Because it takes place in the spring, Passover is sometimes called the Jewish Easter. This is less ridiculous than the misreading of Hannukah as the Jewish Christmas, for the Last Supper in the passion story is identified as a Passover meal. The original connection between the two feasts is preserved in the terms for Easter that have evolved in the Romance languages: *Pacques* in French, *Pascua* in Spanish, and *Pasqua* in Italian.

MAY DAY

In preindustrial Europe, the first of May was widely celebrated as the beginning of warm weather and natural fruition. The Romans held games in honor of the goddess of flowers around this date, and the Druids lit new fires in honor of the god Bel. In the Middle Ages most European communities celebrated May by decorating their homes with new flowers (the custom of carrying in baskets of flowers was known as "bringing in the May"), choosing a Queen of the May, and erecting and dancing around a Maypole. It was the Maypole, with its phallic and pagan connotations, that brought May Day into disrepute among the seventeenth-century Puritans. In both Old and New England the custom of dancing around the Maypole was outlawed by the religious authorities.

The rise of industrial capitalism made the holiday seem atavistic as well as irreligious. It lost its former popularity, except in isolated localities, and today our May Day celebrations, where they exist at all, recall political rather than natural events. Since 1889, when the French-based Second International renamed it Labor Day, May 1 has been the purely secular holiday of European (and some American) socialists. May Days throughout Europe (most visibly in the Soviet Union) are vast celebrations of working-class solidarity, rife with banner-rich parades and anticapitalist oratory. It's ironic that the United States lacks similar celebrations, for May Day was chosen as labor's holiday in the first place to commemorate the labor rally on May 1, 1886, in Chicago that led to the infamous Haymarket Riot and the subsequent decimation of the labor anarchist movement.

MOTHER'S DAY

Although attempts have been made to link Mother's Day to ancient cults of the mother goddess, especially the worship of Cybele, the association is more conceptual than historic. Mother's Day is a modern, American invention. Its creator was Anna M. Jarvis (1864–1948), a West Virginia schoolteacher whose lifelong devotion to her own mother was augmented by what she saw as the ill treatment of many elders by their children. When her mother died in 1905, Jarvis undertook a letter-writing campaign, petitioning ministers, businessmen, and congressmen to support the idea of a national day set aside to honor mothers. Three years later, her persistence paid off, as churches in her hometown of Grafton and in Philadelphia, where she then lived, held observances on May 10, one day after the anniversary of her mother's death. In 1910, West Virginia became the first state to proclaim a national day of observance, and within a year the rest of the union followed suit. Anna Jarvis was fifty years old, in 1914, when she saw her project become a national holiday: In that year President Woodrow Wilson established the second Sunday in May as the date.

MEMORIAL DAY

Today's Memorial Day events—the parades, the oratorical elegies, the wreath-layings—honor the dead of all wars; but the prototype of the holiday recalled the victims of the Civil War. The year was 1866, and the place the little village of Waterloo, in the Finger Lakes region of New York. According to holiday historian Robert Myers, the man behind the idea was Henry C. Welles, a druggist who suggested to a veterans organization that the graves of the dead be decorated with flowers. Decoration Day was born of that idea, and it was celebrated for the first time on May 5. The Grand Army of the Republic, the Union vets' principal support group, picked up on the Waterloo celebrations and spread the idea throughout the country. Beginning with New York state in 1873, an increasing number of states have made it a legal holiday, until today it is a de facto national celebration.

FATHER'S DAY

Father's Day was started as a reaction, or perhaps as an afterthought, to Mother's Day. Not only was the first Father's Day service held in Fairmont, West Virginia, in July 1908 (just two months after and twenty miles down the river from the first Mother's Day in Grafton), but the woman chiefly responsible for popularizing the celebration, Mrs. John Bruce of Spokane, got the idea while listening to a Mother's Day sermon. That was in 1909, and by the following year she had persuaded the Spokane city fathers to observe one Sunday in June as an official tribute to paternity. Her original choice was June 5, the birthday of her father, who had raised six children after the death of his wife, but the third Sunday proved logistically more acceptable, and so it has stayed ever since.

Although fathers were widely honored on that day beginning early in the century, and although President Wilson endorsed it as he had Mother's Day, the legal parity of the paternal holiday was slow in coming. For over sixty years, American presidents had to make annual ad hoc proclamations, for Congress was strangely reluctant—a rare instance of modesty, perhaps—to give Dad an equal, permanent footing with Mom. It wasn't until 1972 that Congress established the national holiday.

THE OLD-FASHIONED FOURTH

The fireworks extravaganza that capped the Liberty Weekend celebration of the Statue of Liberty centennial in 1986 was widely mocked as glitzy and Hollywoodesque, but in fairness to the festival's promoters, it should be pointed out that they were only extending to its logical absurdity a 200-year-old tradition. The old-fashioned Fourth that our oldest citizens remember consisted not only of the oratory that has now largely disappeared but also of the sparklers and firecrackers that have remained, and the practice of celebrating Independence Day with such devices goes back almost to its beginning.

When the colonies voted for independence on July 2, 1776, John Adams wrote to his wife that the day ought henceforth to be "solemnized with pomp and parade, with shows, games and sport, guns, bells, bonfires and illuminations, from one end of this continent to the other, from this time forward, forevermore." He was getting a little ahead of Manifest Destiny with that bit about both ends of the continent, and it turned out he had the date wrong, since the day of adoption, July 4, would ultimately be chosen. But in his hyperbolic zeal to commemorate independence, Adams had a lot of the details right. The most characteristic and lasting feature of the modern Fourth—the twilight fireworks display—grows out of the gunfire, bonfires, and "illuminations" that he so fervently hoped for.

LABOR DAY

The picnics, speeches, and parades of today's Labor Day were all part of the first celebration, held in New York City in 1882. Its promoter was an Irish–American labor leader named Peter J. McGuire. A carpenter by trade, McGuire had worked since the age of eleven, and in 1882 was president of the United Brotherhood of Carpenters and Joiners. Approaching the city's Central Labor Union that summer, he proposed a holiday that would applaud "the industrial spirit—the great vital force of every nation." On September 5 his suggestion bore fruit, as an estimated 10,000 workers, many of them bucking their bosses' warnings, left work to march from Union Square up Fifth Avenue to 42nd Street. The event gained national attention, and by 1893 thirty states had made Labor Day an annual holiday.

The quick adoption of the scheme may have indicated less about the state legislators' respect for working people than about a fear of risking their ire. In the 1880s the United States was a land sharply divided between the immensely wealthy and the very poor. The utopian socialist Henry George was accurate in describing the era as one of "progress and poverty." In a society in which factory owners rode in private Pullmans while ten-year-olds slaved in the mines, anticapitalist resentment ran high. Demands for radical change were common throughout the labor press. With socialists demanding an end to "wage slavery" and anarchists extolling the virtues of dynamite, middle-of-the-roaders like Samuel Gompers and McGuire seemed attractively mild by comparison. One can imagine pragmatic capitalists seeing Labor Day as a bargain: A one-day party certainly cost them less than paying their workers decent wages.

HALLOWEEN TRICK-OR-TREATING

Samhain was an ancient Celtic New Year's festival during which human and animal sacrifices were made to the Lord of the Dead (called Saman) and the sun. Celebrated on November 1, Samhain is the original of our Halloween, although the modern holiday also reflects the influence of medieval churchmen, particularly Pope Gregory III, who in the eighth century designated November 1 as the feast of departed Christian saints. It is as the eve of All Hallows Day, or "Hallow's e'en," that we now observe October 31.

The fascination with witches and the dead exhibited on that day may be traced to both the pagan and the Christian holidays, and so, possibly, may the secular tradition of trick-or-treating. Robert Myers traces the practice to Samhain, when, after offering a feast to the dead, "masked and costumed villagers representing the souls of the

dead paraded to the outskirts of town leading the ghosts away." A
later Christian contribution can be found in medieval All Hallows
processions, in which relics of saints were displayed and parishoners
dressed as their favorites. There is also a possible connection with the
Guy Fawkes celebrations of post-Renaissance England. In these,
youngsters dressed up as the executed conspirator to beg "a penny
for the Guy" from passing strangers.

Given the Celtic origin of the holiday, however, the most appealing of explanations may be one given by Ralph and Adelin Linton.
A traditional Irish custom on Samhain eve, they say, was the solicit-
ing of contributions in the name of Muck Olla, a shadowy and
probably Druidic figure who, so the solicitors promised potential
donors, would be sure to wreak vengeance on the ungenerous. Muck
Olla's vengeance gradually became transformed into that of slighted
fairies and goblins, and ultimately into the tricks of disappointed
human revelers.

JACK O'LANTERNS

O'Lantern sounds Irish, and it is. The flickering, carved pumpkin
faces that animate the American Halloween derive from an old Irish
custom of creating rustic lanterns from vegetables. The Irish child's
typical Halloween flashlight was a hollowed-out turnip or potato
with a candle inside, and when the Irish landed in America in the
nineteenth century, they were quick to spot the possibilities in the
pumpkin.

The hollowed-out vegetables got their name because of the tale of
one Jack, a notoriously stingy tippler who nearly lost his soul one
Halloween night when he chanced upon the Devil in a pub. Many
more than one over the eight, Jack was about to expire and Old Nick
about to claim his doomed spirit, when he managed to convince the
Devil that, if he could have one last drink, he would follow him
happily to Hades. "The trouble is I have no more money," Jack
implored. "So if you'll just change yourself into sixpence, I can have
my drink, and we can be on our way." The Devil, happy to demonstrate his shape-shifting prowess, obliged. Jack popped him into a
purse and refused to let him out until he promised not to claim his
soul for ten years.

That wasn't the end of the story. Ten years later, Jack was walking in the country near an orchard when Old Nick came to collect. But Jack had another ruse up his sleeve. "Before you carry me off to perdition," he asked the Devil, "would you be the gentleman I've heard that you are and fetch me one of those apples? You can stand on my shoulders to reach it." The Devil, who had learned little from their last encounter, climbed upon Jack's shoulders, whereupon Jack whipped out a penknife and carved a cross in the trunk of the tree. This left the Devil in the air, and as a condition of getting him down, Jack made him promise that he would never again ask for his soul. And the Devil, double-crossed, had to promise.

But, of course, he had the last laugh. When Jack finally died, he was turned away from Heaven for his sins, and when he then applied for entrance to Hell, the Devil said, "I cannot break my word." So poor Jack had nowhere to go and was condemned to become a kind of Celtic wandering Jew. "Give me at least a light to find my way," he pleaded with the Devil, and in this the Devil obliged him, by hurling in his direction a coal from the fires of Hell. According to tradition, Jack placed it inside a turnip he had been munching, and the jack o'lantern was born.

THE THANKSGIVING TURKEY

Why do Americans eat turkey at Thanksgiving? Not because of the Pilgrims. Turkeys were probably eaten at the famous "first Thanksgiving" in 1621, but there is no hard evidence. Colonial records mention only "fowl" and deer, the latter supplied by the Indians. Turkey did not become customary Thanksgiving Day fare until the turn of the nineteenth century, and it did not become the traditional main course until the 1860s. Moreover, the Turkey Day tradition became firmly established only after World War II, thanks to an aggressive marketing campaign on the part of the poultry industry. That effort, which coexisted with the development of hybrid gobblers, helped to invent the supposed Pilgrim tradition and successfully made the stuffed bird an image of American abundance.

Like the turkey, Thanksgiving itself is a relatively young American tradition. It stems from the very ancient harvest feast and has a more immediate connection with the Harvest Home ceremonies of the Pilgrims' England. But thanksgivings were intermittent in America until 1863. For the previous four decades the indomitable Sarah Josepha Hale, editor of *Godey's Lady's Book,* had waged a one-woman campaign for a regular, national holiday. In 1863 her efforts bore fruit, when President Lincoln declared that the last Thursday in November would thereafter be Thanksgiving Day.

HANNUKAH LIGHTS

In 165 B.C. Jewish revolutionaries under Judas Maccabeus succeeded in driving from Jerusalem the occupying army of the Syrian king Antiochus IV. In his subsequent rededication of the temple, Judas could find enough undefiled oil to light the sacred lamps for only one day, but miraculously they burned for eight days. In remembrance of this political and religious victory, Jews light the eight-branched *menorah,* or candelabrum, at the annual feast known as Hannukah, or "Dedication." On the first night of the eight-day celebration a single candle is lit, on the second, two, and so forth, until all eight are burning in commemoration.

Because it takes place in December and because children are given presents at the candle-lightings, Hannukah is often referred to, by Gentiles, not as the Feast of Lights, but as the Jewish Christmas. Aside from the possible connection that Christmas and Hannukah may have to prehistoric solstice rites, the two holidays are not related. Nor does Hannukah play anywhere near the important role in the Jewish year as Christmas does in the Christian.

XMAS

This common abbreviation for *Christmas* might easily be interpreted as an instance of modern insolence, or laziness, or both, and I remember, during my Catholic boyhood, being told by a more pious acquaintance that to write an "X" for Christ's name was a gross insult, if not sacrilege. Actually he was both overzealous and wrong, for the letter "X" in Xmas, like the letter alone as a sign for a kiss, stands quite appropriately for the name Christ. In Greek, it's the first letter, transliterated *chi,* of Jesus' name. The abbreviation isn't modern, either. The *Oxford English Dictionary* mentions a somewhat longer version, *X'temmas,* dating from 1551.

THE CHRISTMAS TREE

The Christmas tree, like the Maypole, originated ultimately in pre-Christian Europe, where the northern peoples believed that trees (fruit trees and evergreens in particular) were embodiments of powerful beings. This connection to paganism is distant, however, and the more immediate link is to the Middle Ages. In the fourteenth and fifteenth centuries, Phillip V. Snyder notes, the designated miracle play for December 24 was the story of Adam and Eve, and in this play the chief prop was an apple-hung evergreen called the paradise tree, dramatically evoking, for the illiterate medieval audiences, the lost innocence of Eden. Perhaps as an invitation to that innocence, perhaps as a throwback to their pagan heritage, German families in the sixteenth century began bringing evergreens into their homes during the holiday season. By the seventeenth century, these were known as *Christbaüme* ("Christ trees") and were being decorated with fruit, candies, cookies, and flat wafers resembling the eucharistic host. The candles that were the precursors of our Christmas lights were introduced at about the same time—although a pretty but unsubstantiated legend says they were invented earlier by Martin Luther.

The *Christbaum* remained largely a German custom until the nineteenth century, when it was taken to England by German merchants and popularized by Victoria's beloved consort, Prince Albert of Saxe-Coburg. The first Christmas trees in America were set up by German immigrants in the 1820s, although it was many decades before the custom took firm hold. As late as 1878, according to Snyder, one New York reporter referred to the import as "an aboriginal oddity." The almost universal adoption of the custom, Snyder says, dates from the 1910s.

RED AND GREEN FOR CHRISTMAS

The dominant color scheme of the holiday season reflects the ancient popularity of holly among both the Britons and the Romans. Holly, like other evergreens, was commonly used as winter decoration in the hope that the plant's remarkable ability to survive throughout the "death" of winter would lend a similar strength to people's homes. During the Roman Saturnalia, berried holly was placed in windows, T. G. Crippen suggests, as an offer of hospitality to the spirits of the then-denuded woods, and the second-century Christian writer Tertullian complained that his fellow religionists did the same. Whatever the reason the custom was originally adopted, it proved easily assimilable into Christian iconography, for two reasons. First, the holly bush could be (and was) likened to the burning bush of the Old Testament. Second, with its prickles and blood-red berries, the plant was a tailor-made emblem of the crown of thorns that Jesus would eventually wear.

The red and green poinsettia, native to Central America, has been a Christmas symbol in the United States since the 1820s, when it was first shipped north by Joel Poinsett, the American minister to Mexico. Its shape is frequently compared to the mythically symmetrical Star of Bethlehem.

KISSING UNDER THE MISTLETOE

Among the Druids of pre-Christian Britain, mistletoe was a sacred, medicinal herb, so esteemed for its curative properties that it was popularly known as *all-heal.* Sir James Frazer identified it as the golden bough plucked by Aeneas from the oak at the gate of the underworld, and the Druids seem to have been no less fascinated by its magic than the Romans: A Druid priest who removed a sprig from its host plant, the oak, had to do so with a golden sickle and catch it in a white cloth before it hit the ground. The only bad news we hear of the mistletoe in ancient times is that it was used in a dart to kill Balder, the most beloved and innocent of the Norse gods; but even this reinforces the plant's reputation for having magical power over life and death.

Frazer associates the kissing custom with the "license of the Greek

Saturnalia," and Philip Waterman, casting still further, sees it as a survival of temple prostitution in the worship of the "Babylonian Venus," Mylitta. T. G. Crippen, who sees it as a "peculiarly English" custom, makes a couple of better guesses. It may reflect a primitive marriage or fertility rite. Or it may go back to a Scandinavian truce custom. If people were prohibited from fighting when they met near mistletoe in the forest, it may have been but a short step to the custom of hanging a sprig on a doorway "to imply a pledge of peace and friendship" that would "be sealed with a friendly greeting" like a kiss. This would make the Christmas connection logical, since it is the season of peace.

NATIVITY SCENES

Perhaps because it so vividly illustrates the importance to Christianity of "holy poverty," the nativity scene has been a popular icon to the faithful for many hundreds of years. Francis Weiser (1952) says that the first known depiction of the nativity scene, found in the catacombs of Rome, dates from A.D. 380. The first three-dimensional depiction, however—that is, the first example of what we would call a crèche, or manger display—is traditionally attributed to St. Francis, the thirteenth-century Italian monk who made poverty and saintliness seem synonymous. Francis conceived the idea of a public manger display in 1223 and persuaded a wealthy nobleman, Giovanni Velitta, to fund the project in the town of Greccio. That first scene contained live animals, actors who played Mary, Joseph, and the shepherds, and a wax figure for *il Bambino*. It was extremely well-received by the peasantry, who no doubt appreciated not just the theatrics but the fact that the straw used in the display was later credited with curative powers. From Greccio, near Francis's hometown of Assissi, the custom spread throughout Italy and then Europe.

CAROLING

The word *carol,* like *choral* and *chorus,* referred originally not to song but to dance. Francis Weiser (1952) says that ring dances, performed to flute music, were popular among the ancient Greeks and Romans, and were brought by the latter to England, where they remained popular into medieval times. By the thirteenth century in that country, *carol* had come to mean not just the dance, but the music that was sung to accompany it, and today only this secondary meaning remains.

The association of joyous song with Christmas dates back, according to legend, to St. Francis. Although he evidently did not compose vernacular songs himself, he is supposed to have led the singing at the nativity scene that he set up as the first public crèche, in Greccio. He did write a Latin hymn, "Psalmus in Nativitate." Christmas songs spread from Italy throughout Europe and enjoyed great popularity until the Reformation, when they ran afoul of puritan austerity. During the seventeenth-century ban on such levity, many of the old carols were lost, and as a result many that we sing today date from the eighteenth-century Methodist revival or later. "Hark, the Herald Angels Sing," for example, was written by Charles Wesley himself. "Joy to the World" came from English poet Isaac Watts in 1748. The American carols "It Came Upon the Midnight Clear," "O Little Town of Bethlehem," and "We Three Kings" are all nineteenth-century creations. So too are the French "O Holy Night" and what is probably the quintessential carol, the German "Silent Night."

YULE LOG

The traditional English Christmas included the burning of a massive Yule log that had been ceremoniously dragged in by many hands and placed on the hearth on Christmas Eve. The mundane reason for the custom was to keep chilly English houses warm, but there was a ritualistic aspect to it as well. "Yule" (in Anglo-Saxon, *geol*) was the winter solstice period in pagan England, and the burning of a huge log at this time was part of the ceremonies that honored the return of the sun. In a classic instance of sympathetic magic, the ancient Celtic and Teutonic peoples would light the log as both a register and an assurance of heavenly light. The cyclical nature of the custom was enshrined in the later folk belief that each year's Yule log should be lighted from the relit remnant of the last year's.

Other folk beliefs attended the log ceremony. T. G. Crippen mentions, for example, the notion that girls with unwashed hands who touched the log would cause the fire to burn dully and the more common superstition that all who helped drag in the behemoth would be protected from witchcraft for a year. There was also the strange practice of drawing a chalk man on the log before it was put to the flame—a recollection, perhaps, of human sacrifice.

CANDLES IN THE WINDOW

Candles have been used for devotional purposes as far back as Biblical times, and it is likely that the Christian fondness for them was inherited from the Hebrews, by way of Rome. The Jewish Feast of Lights at Hannukah and the Roman use of candles at the Saturnalia may both have set a precedent for Christmas tapers. At any rate Christian mythology easily assimilated the symbolic value of candles. Durandus, an early Church writer, said that the wax of a candle represented Christ's body, the wick his soul, and the flame his imperishable, divine nature. And as T. G. Crippen points out, the large, long-lasting Christmas candle that became popular during the Middle Ages was likened both to the star of Bethlehem, and to Jesus himself, as the "light of the world."

The candles that we place in windows at the Christmas season probably derive from the medieval Christmas candle, but there are also two interesting social explanations. Folklorist Maria Leach (1954) explains the custom as a kind of outreach rite: The lights in the windows are meant to light the Christ child to shelter, or to welcome his symbolic heirs, weary travelers. Francis Weiser (1952) offers a political explanation. The custom, he says, was brought to America by the Irish, who initiated it while under British rule. In early days priests were inherently suspect, because they represented a religious rival to the Crown, and the candles were placed in windows at the Christmas season in the hope of attracting fugitive clerics to come in and say Mass. The "light for the Christ child" story, Weiser says, was a tale to throw the English off the track.

CHRISTMAS "CHEER"

The popularity of cups of cheer at Christmastime goes back to the old English custom of wassailing, which the *Oxford English Dictionary* defines as "carousing" or "riotous festivity." The term *wassail* is a form of the Middle English *waes haeil,* which means "be in good health." From about the thirteenth century it was used not only as a toast but also as the name of the traditional Christmas beverage. This was a mixture of ale, roasted apples, sugar, and spices, with eggs or cream sometimes added. Served hot from giant "wassail bowls," it remained the favorite English brew until the early part of the eighteenth century, when the growing popularity of spirits brought punch into favor. Today, of course, liquor-based punches, not to mention egg nogs (a nineteenth-century invention) have all but replaced the original wassail, and only the toast remains.

CHRISTMAS STOCKINGS

The custom of hanging stockings on a mantel in anticipation of small presents is believed to have started as a kind of mercenary homage to St. Nicholas, the Turkish progenitor of our Santa Claus. Of the many stories told about the kindness of St. Nick, one very popular one has him providing dowries for the three daughters of an impoverished nobleman by throwing bags of money through their windows or, in some versions of the tale, dropping them down the chimney. As Maymie Krythe (1954) recounts the story, one of these down-the-chimney gifts happened to fall into a stocking that was hung to dry by the fire; hence our custom of hanging stockings in the same place.

CHRISTMAS CARDS

Although there are probably more Christmas cards sent today than valentines, the former have a much shorter history. The sending of Yuletide greetings in America did not become popular until the 1870s, when the German lithographer Louis Prang began producing Christmas cards in Boston. His beautifully crafted creations—big on sentiment and flowers as well as Christmas scenes—dominated the market until the 1890s, when his near-monopoly was eroded by cheap imports from his native Germany. Prang cards are still prized by collectors.

Before Prang, there was John Calcott Horsley, an English artist who is generally considered the creator of the first Christmas card, or at least the first one available for commercial consumption. Robert Myers says that this innovation took place in 1843, at the request of one Henry Cole, and this first card sold perhaps a thousand copies at a shilling each. Considering the billions (yes, billions) of cards that are exchanged each Christmas these days, this was a pretty small affair, but in terms of design the basics were there. Horsley's first showed a family at a Christmas feast. The soon-to-be-classic inscription was "Merry Christmas and a Happy New Year to You."

CHRISTMAS GIFTS

The custom of exchanging presents at Christmas is commonly linked to the Magi's visit to the infant Jesus and their gifts to him of gold, frankincense, and myrrh. Actually, gift-giving at the time of the winter solstice was a Roman custom before Jesus' time. Suetonius called the Romans' traditional winter gifts *strenae,* and the term (as well as the custom) is preserved in the French *étrenne* ("New Year's gift"). Most *strenae* had a largely symbolic significance: Maymie Krythe (1954) notes that honey, fruits, and lamps were among the popular choices, although gold coins were also sometimes given. Alms-giving may also be traced to this period, since at the Roman Saturnalia the wealthy were obliged to share with the poor.

The American version of this custom, however, is only conceptually related to Rome. The nearer models for what James Barnett cleverly calls our Big Swap are the generosity of the proto-Santa, St. Nicholas, and the gifts that many Europeans believe the baby Jesus brings on his birthday. The objects bestowed by both these gift-bringers were, like the Roman gifts, of a nominal nature; the lavish exchanges of this century are a relatively recent innovation. They began around the same time as the modern Santa, as part of the nineteenth-century commercialization of the holiday.

GIFT-WRAPPING

The wrapping of Christmas presents, William Waits notes, is a fairly recent phenomenon in American life. It arose at the turn of the century, during a period when handmade presents were giving way to machine-made, store-bought ones. For both givers and manufacturers, this shift presented a problem, for the machine-made items, precisely because they were convenient, represented less of the giver's personal attention than the hand-made items had done; thus they were symbolically less intimate. To disguise this loss of symbolic value, and to invest the manufactured items with a personal touch, retailers encouraged shoppers to have their purchases gift-wrapped. Gift-wrapping, in Waits's acute term, became a "decontaminating mechanism" that removed the presents from the "normal flow of bought-and-sold goods" and made them, for a single ceremonial moment, emblems of intimacy rather than commerce.

SANTA CLAUS

The American Santa Claus is the latest step in a legend that began in the fourth century in Asia Minor. The prototype of the Christmas gift-bringer was the bishop of Myra, St. Nicholas, who was universally loved for his generosity and who today remains a principal saint of the Eastern Church. Dressed in bishop's garb and sporting a long white beard, he is supposed to have left good children presents on his feast day, December 6. Reformation zealots banished this homey character from the Church calendar, and he was widely replaced by the Christmas Man, a secular Yuletide supplier known in England as Father Christmas and in France as Père Noel. But Nicholas had been the patron of sailors as well as of children, and the seagoing Dutch kept him on in spite of their Calvinist leanings. In the Netherlands he was called Sint Nikolaas or simply Sinterklaas. It was as Sinterklaas that he entered the New World.

Santa Claus as we know him today was the offspring of a theologian and a cartoonist. The theologian, Dr. Clement C. Moore, was the author in 1822 of the immensely popular poem "A Visit from St. Nicholas," also known as "The Night Before Christmas," which presented the recent Dutch import as a toy-toting pipe smoker, the driver of a reindeer-drawn sleigh, and a fancier of chimneys. It's not clear which of these elements were Moore's own and which he borrowed from the stories of Dutch friends. The cartoonist was Thomas Nast of *Harper's Weekly*. His illustrations of Santa for that paper, done in the two decades after the Civil War, established the image of the robust character we know today. (Nast, incidentally, also gave us the Democrats' donkey and the Republicans' elephant.)

RUDOLPH THE RED-NOSED REINDEER

The story of Rudolph, the reindeer whose shiny nose lights Santa Claus's way "one foggy Christmas eve," is as well known to American children as the story of Santa himself. Its popularity is the result partly of the fact that it is, in sociologist James Barnett's description, "the only original addition to the folklore of Santa Claus in the century," and partly to the fact that, as a variation on the ugly duckling motif, it addresses children's innate confusion about social roles. The "lesson" of the Rudolph tale is a necessary and comforting one: Whoever you are, you are special.

The story was created in 1939 by a Montgomery Ward adman named Robert May, known throughout the firm for his light verse. Seeking something that their store Santas could hand out to children, company managers asked May for a poem. With the editorial advice of his four-year-old daughter, he came up with Rudolph and his nose. That first year, 2.4 million copies, illustrated by May's friend Denver Gillen, were distributed in Montgomery Ward stores. World War II stopped Rudolph's rounds, but they picked up again in 1946, and a year later the poem appeared in book form. In 1949 the red-nosed charmer's career really took off, when singing cowboy star Gene Autry recorded Johnny Marks's musical version and propelled it to the top of the Hit Parade. Soon Rudolph was appearing on television and was on his way to becoming an institution.

CHARMED, I'M SURE:

SUPERSTITIONS

HORSESHOES

Since at least the days of the Romans, horseshoes have been considered lucky, both for their healing powers (Pliny says they can cure hiccups) and for their protective influence (specifically, against witches). Robert Lawrence says that the horseshoe usually is placed above doorways and gives over a dozen reasons for its popularity. Many of these are fanciful, but at least three are worth considering.

In the most convincing explanation, the horseshoe is a horn-shaped amulet that resembles the crescent moon. Frederick Elworthy says both the horseshoe and the Mediterranean *mano cornuta,* or "horned hand" sign, are protections against the evil eye, and Lawrence mentions similar-shaped charms in use among the Chaldeans and Egyptians. The awe in which primitive people must have held the moon, which periodically "dies" and is "reborn," certainly influenced their fascination with this shape.

Lawrence also mentions the "time-honored belief in the magical power of iron" and suggests that the metal itself may have contributed to the horseshoe's use as a charm. Ancient blacksmiths, performing a kind of crude alchemy, were often identified as sorcerers. This fact, along with the supposed efficacy of fire as a bane to demons, helps to support the "magical iron" explanation.

In a third explanation, the horseshoe is related to animal worship. Both the horse and the serpent were objects of worship in ancient Europe, and both were frequently connected to the infernal spirits that an amulet might keep at bay. Remember also that the horseshoe approaches the form of the serpent biting its own tail—a universally beneficent symbol of eternity.

FOUR-LEAF CLOVERS

Clover has long been used in folk medicine. E. and M. A. Radford call it one of the "anti-witch plants" of the Middle Ages; herbalists have recommended it for cleansing the blood, healing sores, and quieting coughs. Writers on the superstition agree that its origins are "lost in antiquity," but George Stimpson (1948) makes the sensible guess that the good luck is associated with the clover's shape, similar to that of the Christian cross. The belief also may have something to do with popular awe at the sports of nature (a four-leaf clover is a mutant three-leaf). Along with the fearful distaste that people commonly bring to things novel in behavior or appearance is often an element of nervous respect. (Thus epilepsy was regarded histori-cally as a "sacred" affliction, and infants born with a caul were thought, in American folklore, to possess powers of "second sight.") The respect paid the sportive four-leaf clover may display this same mixture of attitudes.

BLACK CATS

In most of the witch-hunting crazes that afflicted Europe between the Middle Ages and the eighteenth century, the victimized "witches" were typically older women whose crimes were eccen-tricity, solitude, and mortal weakness—specifically, the inability to withstand the public ordeals that "proved" them to be guilty of wrongdoing. In this frenzy of righteousness, the witch hunters fre-quently bolstered their cases with the hard evidence that Goodwife So-and-So owned a "familiar" or a demon that had assumed the shape of an animal, most commonly a toad or a cat. Suspicion of toads has abated today, but the prejudice against the black cat is a direct survivor of the witch-hunting era. This prejudice continues, as Pennethorne Hughes points out, because old women still keep cats and, it might be added, they are still ranted at by the dimwit-ted as "crones" and "witches." If old women had kept chickens in the Middle Ages, there are some who would now boycott Colonel Sanders.

Interestingly, although black cats are pretty widely held in awe, that awe is not always one of fear. In England black cats are considered lucky, and T. S. Knowlson says this prejudice *for* the animal has existed "from time immemorial."

BROKEN MIRRORS

Mirrors have been used in divination since ancient times; the Greeks called looking-glass divination "catoptromancy." Because of their presumed value in seeing the future, superstition grants them a magical, and potentially dangerous, significance. On the simplest level, breaking a mirror is, as T. S. Knowlson put it, "the destruction of a means of knowing the will of the gods," or, as amended by Lillian Eichler (1924), a signal from the gods that they didn't want you poking into their affairs. Either way, the hint of unseeable hazards was obvious. The Romans believed that the mirror reflected both the inner and the outer health of the viewer. Thus to break a mirror presaged ill health. Eichler ties this in with the superstition about seven years' bad luck, since the Romans also believed that a person's health changed every seven years.

In addition to reflecting the future, however, mirrors also were believed to reflect the person's soul, or true being. Many primitive peoples, in fact, believed that the person's soul actually existed *in* the mirror. Breaking the glass would prevent the soul from reuniting with the body, and misfortune would inevitably result. This belief in the intimate connection between an individual and his mirror image lies behind such superficially different beliefs as the Batuso idea that a crocodile can kill a man by attacking his reflection in water and the modern European notion, popularized by Hollywood, that a vampire, being soulless, cannot see itself in the mirror.

RABBIT'S FOOT

Rabbits and hares have an ambivalent nature in folklore. On the one hand, because they are extremely prolific, they have long been considered symbols of fecundity and new life (see THE EASTER BUNNY).

On the other hand, they live underground and so possess an aura of chthonian mystery that has linked them in European history to darkness and witches and the Devil. Some British country folk's reluctance to kill hares may be based on the traditional belief that they are witches in disguise. There is also a belief that rabbits, thought to be born with their eyes open (actually, it is only hares that are born this way), have the power of the evil eye. The rabbit's-foot superstition reflects these folk beliefs, for owning a talismanic part of this fecund yet mysterious animal could give one a vital connection with powerful forces.

OPENING AN UMBRELLA INDOORS

The umbrella reached England by way of Italy early in the seventeenth century and at that time was employed both as a shield against bad weather and as a shade against the sun. The Italian word *ombrella,* in fact, means "little shade." The superstition against opening umbrellas indoors is a common one in the British Isles, and no doubt it traveled to the New World from there.

That this action would be considered unnecessary or foolish is understandable, but why would it be seen as dangerous? E. and M. A. Radford hint at an origin in sympathetic magic, since "an umbrella unnecessarily opened during fine weather may bring down the rain." Rudolph Brasch provides a more subtle rationale, suggesting that indoor umbrella usage violates "the right order of things" and may thus be seen by the superstitious as a testing of the powers that be. Specifically, such behavior might be seen as insulting to God— who "intended umbrellas to be employed out of doors"—or to "the spirit of the umbrella" itself. A third insultee, I would suggest, would be the spirits of the household, who might be piqued at the implication that their protection must be supplemented by an overhead shield. Of course, simple pragmatism may also enter in: The custom may enshrine a long-forgotten accident in which someone opened an umbrella in his house and knocked over a burning candle or the china.

SAYING "GOD BLESS YOU" TO A SNEEZER

Many peoples around the world are heartened by hearing someone sneeze. Among these sternuphiliacs, or sneeze-lovers, are the Maori of New Zealand, who believe that the creator god Tiki sneezed life into the first human being; the Zulus of southern Africa, who take the sneeze as the sign of a beneficent spirit; and the ancient Hebrews, who identified sneezing with life, because they recognized, as Maria Leach (1954) observed, that "the dead never sneeze." Some American Indian peoples said that a good sneeze clears the brain.

But sternuphilia is by no means universal. In many European cultures, sneezing traditionally is associated with death, and it is to this sternuphobic tradition that Americans generally belong. You are very close to death when you sneeze, it is widely believed, because sneezing can expel the soul, and thus life, from the body. There is a linguistic, if not medical, logic to this superstition, since the Latin word *anima* means both "soul" and "breath of life." So we say "God bless you" to a sneezer as a charm against the danger of the moment. Neglecting this magical utterance could mean that the sneezer would end up in the next world.

SPILLING SALT

Maria Leach (1954) recounts a quaint legend that illustrates the value of salt in ancient times. A king with three daughters asks each of them to describe the depth of her love for him. The first says she loves him as much as bread, the second as much as wine, and the third as much as salt. Offended at being likened to such a common substance as salt, the king banishes the third daughter from his presence. She stays banished until, conspiring with the palace cook, she arranges a completely saltless meal for her father. At this point, the monarch sees the light, admits he cannot live without salt, and calls her back.

The story is Roman in origin, but it reflects the importance of salt throughout the ancient world. Because of its value as a preservative, antiseptic, and flavoring, salt was considered almost supernatural.

Among Greeks, Romans, and Hebrews it was a common sacrificial offering. Throughout the Middle East, moreover, it was a token of friendship and trust. Spilling such an honored substance was seen as an affront to the celestial powers; the association of spilled salt with bad luck is therefore of great antiquity. It did not arise, as has often been stated, with Leonardo da Vinci's *Last Supper*, where Judas has knocked over the salt cellar; in this, Leonardo was mirroring an old tradition.

One may counteract the effect of spilled salt by throwing a little over the left shoulder. Robert Lawrence remarks that this gesture may be seen as either conciliatory or confounding. The thrown salt may serve as an informal sacrifice, or it may be an attack on the evil spirits who are thought to have caused the spilling in the first place. Central European folklore says that the Devil cannot abide salt; so the left-shoulder ploy may be a way "to hit the invisible Devil in the eye." It's the left shoulder because, as Robert Hertz first pointed out, the right hand is associated with what is "right"; the left represents "the perpetual menace of evil."

"BREAK A LEG"

This is the traditional good luck wish to an actor about to go on. The oddity of the pronouncement is explained by the logic of paranoia. Among highly superstitious theater people, it is thought that wishing for good luck will inevitably backfire—so you wish for bad luck instead and hope that Dame Fortune will cue you.

Although he doesn't mention the fractured femur injunction, T. S. Knowlson lists other beliefs that attest to the superstitiousness of actors. It is good luck, for example, to have your shoes squeak during an entrance, and it is good luck to have a theater cat. But bad luck comes from all directions: from whistling in the theater, from repeating the last line of a play at rehearsal, from "certain shades of yellow," and—horror of thespian horrors—from being forced to do a scene on a set with a picture of an ostrich. One can imagine Gielgud losing sleep over that one.

Knowlson attributes these traditional fears to the artistic temperament, that psychology so "full of weird possibilities." It's more likely that they have to do with mere stage fright, with the contempt in which acting was held until quite recent times, and with the notorious instability of the profession. When your livelihood depends on satisfying the public whim by pretending to be someone you are not, it's no wonder you're always expecting disaster.

WALKING UNDER A LADDER

Avoiding ladders used to be linked to the story of the crucifixion: One kept one's distance, on pain of incurring bad luck, from the instrument that had taken Jesus down from the cross. This is highly suspect reasoning, since none of the four Gospels even mentions a ladder. The superstition has also been linked to the fear of entering the Holy Trinity's emblematic triangle, formed by ladder, wall, and ground (why wouldn't doing that bring *good* luck?). And with a logic that is even less coherent, the superstition has been linked to primitive menstrual taboos. The plain and quite rational rationale for not walking under a ladder is that in going around it, you are less likely to be rained on by paint or hammers.

KNOCKING ON WOOD

The English touch wood for luck; Americans prefer the more brazen knock. These actions are variations on a motif, and many suggest that the motif reflects the early Christian reverence for the cross. Making contact with wood is a way of connecting symbolically with this most potent of Christian talismans. Others see the custom as a survivor of the medieval tradition of sanctuary. In the days when any fugitive could find protection behind the doors of a church, touching the wood of those doors would be a hunted man's signal that he was safe.

These Christian explanations of wood touching, however, may be additions to an older rationale. Tree worship was common in pre-Christian Europe. Oak trees, especially, were widely venerated, from Celtic Britain to the eastern Mediterranean. Yggdrasill, the giant ash tree at the center of the world, served much the same symbolic function among the pagan Norse as the wooden cross has always served for Christians. It provided a fundamental embodiment of life's mysteries by bridging the worlds of the sacred and the profane. Knocking wood for luck, therefore, was the equivalent, long before the Christian era, of knocking on heaven's door.

WISHBONES

The superstition about wishbones—that good luck will follow the person who ends up with the larger "half"—may go back to ancient Rome. Birds were extremely important in Roman divination. A common Latin term for "soothsayer" was *auspex,* which is literally "one who looks at birds" and which gives us our adjective "auspicious." Another related term was *haruspex,* or "one who looks at the entrails" (of birds). While, strictly speaking, bones would not be included in entrails, the soothsayer could hardly miss them during the dissection. In addition, the Old World folkloric custom of gambling by "throwing the bones" (a forerunner of throwing the dice) also hints at an ancient connection between avian bones and divination. It is conceivable, therefore, that the position of the wishbone or technically the *furcula* (which is Latin for "little fork") played some part in the haruspex's prognostications.

BURNING EARS

When someone is speaking ill of another out of that person's hearing, it is said that his ears are burning or tingling; conversely, the superstitious suppose that when their ears burn, it is a sign of some distant malevolence. Pliny wrote about this belief in the first century A.D. He explained the "phenomenon" by reference to a kind of universal fluid that could "touch" an ear at a distance, even though it was out of range of hearing. The more common-sense explanation seems a better one. When someone yells at or insults you in your presence, it makes metaphoric sense to say that he has "burned" your ears. It may even make anatomical sense, since when we are rebuked, we frequently blush with embarrassment. Reasoning backwards by false analogy, then, we can assume that ear burning always has the same cause and that words spoken about us in the next town can embarrass us just as much as those spoken to our faces.

SPITTING FOR LUCK

Huck Finn, who knew (and believed) every superstition in the book, swore by the custom of spitting for luck, and so have many Europeans. Pliny mentioned it, as early as the first century A.D., as a means of averting witchcraft. His contemporary Tacitus reported that spittle had medicinal as well as charm value: The emperor Vespasian, he claimed, once restored sight to a blind man by applying spit to his eyes. Both Mark and John in the New Testament claim the same feat for Jesus. Like all body fluids, spit was powerful, at least in the minds of the ancients, and it was from the belief that it could cure that the spitting superstition no doubt arose.

Incidentally, the supposedly curative power of spittle may not be merely folk legend. Some biologists suggest that animals who lick their wounds do so because their saliva contains certain enzymes that may hasten the clotting of blood. The human custom of kissing a wound to make it better, then, may be only a variation of the older practice of spitting to heal.

TO KILL A MOCKINGBIRD

In naming her 1960 Pulitzer Prize–winning novel *To Kill a Mockingbird,* Harper Lee was evoking the intense hold of custom on small-town life, particularly in the segregated South where she was born. There the fabric of tradition had given rise to the folk belief that it's a sin to kill a mockingbird. (The novel's bitter irony, of course, was that it was not a sin to execute an innocent black.)

There are two likely reasons that the mockingbird might be protected by folk custom throughout the South. One is simply pragmatic: The bird has such a wide mimetic range and such a dulcet tone whatever its copied song, that it would be a "sin" to deprive others of such an inventive creature. The other reason is obliquely political or, more precisely, state-chauvinistic. Because of its polyglottic wizardry, the mockingbird is the state bird of Texas, Mississippi, Tennessee, Florida, and Arkansas. The designated songster of Lee's Alabama is the yellowhammer, but folk traditions are no respecters of state lines. It might be expected that, growing up in mockingbird country, she learned to share with non-Alabaman southerners an affection for this emblem of the region.

HEX SIGNS

Throughout southeastern Pennsylvania, high up near the eaves of old barns, you can see circular designs painted in bright, largely primary colors. Some designs are geometric and some are floral, so that they almost seem to reproduce stylistically the two major decorative traditions of the original inhabitants of the country. But the signs are not Indian in origin. They are the "hex" signs of the Pennsylvania Dutch (that is, "Deutsch," or German) tradition. Spreading out from Berks and Lancaster counties in this century, this evidence of a distinctively American art form may now be seen as far afield as New England.

Experts disagree on the meaning of hex signs. The common view, that they keep evil spirits away from the barns, is discounted by many locals, who say they are simply decorative. Linguistics, on the other hand, argues for the common interpretation. "Hex" is the Americanization of the German *Hexe,* for "witch," and although the term *hex sign* is of fairly recent vintage (before the 1900s, the signs were called flowers or stars), even an after-the-fact association with witchery argues for *some* superstitious resonance. The most common designs on the barns, from their nineteenth-century beginnings, Peter Fossel says, were swastikas, stars, and rosettes—all common mystical symbols in Europe, where the Pennsylvania Dutch came from. Both the swastika and the multirayed star are related to what Rudolph Koch called the "Sun wheel." Six-rayed designs evoke the symbol that Koch calls the Chrismon, or monogram of Christ—a superimposed "I" and "X" for the Greek letters that are the first initials of Jesus and Christ. It seems a safe guess, then, that consciously or not the hex signs are meant to represent power, not merely inessential decor.

FRIDAY THE 13TH

The standard nineteenth-century explanation for the supposed un-luckiness of the number 13 was that there were thirteen at Jesus' Last Supper—Judas was generally thought of as the thirteenth. This widely repeated interpretation led to the fear of the number 13 in general, the specific prohibition against having thirteen at table, and a host of Thirteen Parties at which the superstition was boldly flouted. The supposed malevolence of *Friday* the 13th fit in well, since the Crucifixion took place on that day.

But both fears have pre-Christian roots. The fear of Fridays, ac-cording to William Walsh, may have been connected to the Norse goddess Freya; beginning journeys on that day was considered ill advised because Freya might interpret it as disregard for her day's specialness. The number 13 has been considered special—both for ill and for good—since ancient times. E. and M. A. Radford say the Romans linked the number to "death, destruction, and misfortune." J. E. Cirlot gives it "unfavourable implications" because it is sym-bolic of death and rebirth. And the conventional view of the witch coven is that it had thirteen members.

Common sense is confounded in explaining such number specula-tions, but H.G. Wells (in Eichler, 1924) made a reasonable stab at the puzzle when he noted that twelve incorporates the favorable "triangularity of three and squareness of four"—both these numbers were "good" to the Pythagoreans—but that thirteen cannot be so easily divided. Like eleven, then, thirteen may be suspect on the grounds of its "excessive" nature.

TIDBITS:

A MISCELLANY

NINE-TO-FIVE

We tend to take the eight-hour work day for granted today and speak formulaically of "nine to five" as an equivalent for "time on the job." In fact nine-to-five became the typical day-shift work day only in this century. Federal employees, for example, did not earn the right to a forty-hour work week until the Fair Labor Standards Act of 1938. Indeed, the very idea of an eight-hour work day is barely a hundred years old. Until late in the nineteenth century, a much longer work day was the norm, for children as well as adults. Labor historian Philip Taft notes that, although agitation for an eight-hour day had been carried on "sporadically" by representatives of workers since the Civil War, the first serious proposal for this "radical" reduction in work time was not made until 1884, by the Federation of Organized Trades and Labor Unions. The push for the eight-hour day became one of the principal rallying points for labor in the strike-torn decade of the 1880s. It was a demonstration on behalf of the eight-hour day that led to the infamous Haymarket Riot of 1886, and this objective was also central to the work of Samuel Gompers's A.F. of L., beginning with its 1888 convention.

GROUND-BREAKING

When a site is opened for a new office building or department store, frequently a high public official presides over the opening ceremonies and gets the honor of actually breaking the ground. The fact that he often does so with a shovel that is beribboned and engraved suggests the extent to which he is actually going to be involved in the sweat work. Yet there is a symbolic appropriateness to Mayor Jones breaking the ground. For one thing, since he or she is the paper leader of the legislators and zoning boards who have made the new enterprise possible, the official ground-breaking is a type of symbolic approval. Second, as the political leader of a community, a mayor or governor holds a similar position to that held in earlier times by a village headman or sachem. Just as in many societies, the public land of the people was held legally, as if in trust, by this leader, so it is not unfitting for a modern sachem, in ceremonial garb of top hat and tails, to initiate work on "his" land. Finally, as the "people's representative, it is to his or her advantage to engage publicly in "people's" labor.

CHURCH COLLECTIONS

The traditional collections of modern churches are an outgrowth of two older customs: the offering of sacrifices to a god (as, for example, in the offertory section of the Roman Catholic mass) and the presenting of gifts to a religious leader in addition to, or in lieu of, a salary. William Walsh points out that, in the early days, American ministers were frequently paid in "kind"—tithes to the church consisted of excess grain or slaughtered pigs or cords of wood. As the money economy developed, and as the frontier church spread geographically, cash came to be considered a more appropriate offering, and so the preacher passed his hat rather than filling his wagon. Eventually the hat gave way to the modern collection basket, and in an interesting manner. According to Walsh, the originals of the long-handled baskets were the warming pans that colonial people used to take the chill off their winter sheets, and after these came corn-poppers—as convenient as warming pans in reaching to the far ends of pews, but more decorous in their implementation, since the popper's mesh covering deadened the clink of dropped coins, and thus made it less obvious who was contributing pennies and who pounds. The modern affair is the final, technologically "finished" version of these homier long-handled collection devices; lined with velvet or felt, it is the most decorous of all.

THE TOLLING OF BELLS

Church bells are commonly tolled today to call the faithful to prayer or to celebrate a joyous occasion, such as a feast day or a wedding. William Walsh noted that in earlier times their use was more varied and was as often associated with fear as with joy. Bells came into use in Europe at some time before the seventh century. They were always formally consecrated before being rung, and throughout the Middle Ages they were used to announce the deaths of parishioners (the so-called passing bell), to drive away storms, and to discourage the meddling of evil spirits.

Church bells were also used to rally citizen in times of "tumult," when they were threatened by fire or invaders; thus they prefigured both the fire alarm and the emergency band radio.

GREETING CARDS

The custom of sending greeting cards to friends is not quite 150 years old. We owe its appearance to a British law of 1840 that established inexpensive mail delivery. Before 1840, sending birthday and holiday greetings across the miles was a practice that was largely confined to people who were literate and able to afford private messengers, and there were relatively few of those folks. The 1840 law creating Great Britain's "penny post" opened a market for greeting cards overnight, and London businessman Henry Cole was quick to size up the opportunity. In 1843 he hired artist John Calcott Horsley to design a three-panel card with the message "A Merry Christmas and a Happy New Year to You," and the commercial greeting card was born.

With postage rates still in single figures, and with literacy nourished by public schooling, manufactured cards became extremely popular on both sides of the Atlantic. In America the leading suppliers were Louis Prang, the so-called father of the American Christmas card, and Esther Howland, a specialist in ornate valentines. Their lavish productions dominated the card market until the turn of the century, when the advent of mass-produced penny postcards dramatically shrank the demand. It was as a penny-postcard salesman that Joyce Hall, founder of Hallmark Cards, got his start around 1910. His company has had a corner on the market ever since and has led the way in such other products of the "social expression industry" as gift wrap, stationery, and calendars. Hall's brainchild now pulls in annual sales of about $1 billion.

CHRISTENING A SHIP

The launching of a ship in ancient times was under the supervision of a priest, and among the Romans this official's chief duty was the offering of a *libamentum,* or libation, to the gods. The libation was a small taste of wine that the priest would pour either over the vessel itself or into the waters that would soon receive it, depending on whether the god being honored was the one to whom the ship was consecrated or one of the deities of the sea. The modern custom of breaking a champagne bottle on the prow of a vessel being launched is a survival of this ancient religious practice. Champagne is the required libation today because you do not offer plonk to the gods.

SHIPS AS "SHE"

George Stimpson (1946) provides an amusing explanation of why ships are designated as female. It's because the sailor holds his vessel dear to him and depends on it as he would upon a spouse; "it is natural that he should compare it with woman, man's dearest and most cherished friend, from whom he is often long separated by the nature of his employment." By this logic the soldier would call his rifle she, and likewise the carpenter his hammer. It seems more likely that the femaleness of oceangoing craft has to do with the fact that they embrace and protect their crews, as a mother would her children. Whatever the psychology involved, *ship* is feminine in many languages that assign a gender to nouns, although this is nowhere near being "almost invariably" the case, as Stimpson suggests. Latin *navis* is feminine, for example, as is *nave* in Spanish and Italian. But French *navire* and *batiment* are masculine, and Romance language terminology for *small* ships is "almost invariably" variable: From *el buque* to *la barca* and *el barco;* from *le bateau* to *la barque,* there is considerable confusion over whether boats are female or male.

Only the Germans, pulling no punches, settle the matter through desexing: Both *Schiff* and *Boot* are neuter.

FLAGS AT HALF-MAST

Flags are flown halfway down their poles in many countries as a sign of mourning. As the term *half-mast* indicates, the likely origin of the custom is nautical. In his study of Western naval customs, Leland Lovette writes that in earlier times military vessels indicated a death aboard, as well as the death of a national leader, by slacking off their rigging, trailing their lines, and "cockbilling," or tilting their yard-arms to present a "scandalized" appearance. It was a naval version of sackcloth and ashes, in which sloppiness was a metaphor for sorrow. "The half-masting of colors," he says, "is in reality a survival of the days when a slovenly appearance characterized mourning."

WHITE FLAG FOR TRUCE

That the use of the white flag to ask for a truce is almost universally recognized today is a tribute to Western expansionism, for the symbolism is not traditional around the world. It arose around the eleventh century in Europe, as an emblem of the Peace and Truce of God, an attempt on the part of the medieval Church to curtail the blood lust of the nobility by prohibiting private warfare on weekends, and during Advent and Lent. The injunction was largely ineffective. In 1095 Pope Urban II found a new way to keep his bellicose flock from each others' throats: He set them on Saracen throats instead, by preaching the First Crusade. Since he endorsed the Peace and Truce of God at the same time, those who donned broadswords and mail presumably also packed the white banner.

The rules of war governing the white flag are not as rigid as might be supposed. Circumspection in the presence of a white flag is only prudent because, as flag expert Whitney Smith points out, the device has often been used as a *ruse de guerre*. "Even a temporary halt in battle can give an advantage to the side that is losing; an officer under a truce flag can serve as a spy; and history records numerous and heinous examples of the betrayal of flags of truce." So there is latitude given field commanders who are presented with this offer of peace. They are not in every case bound to honor it.

TRAFFIC LIGHTS

Henry Ford completed his prototype Model T in 1896, and the American romance with the automobile was under way. For the first couple of decades that romance was literally a hit-and-miss affair, because the only traffic control that existed was provided by daredevil cops, who were even less familiar with the capabilities of the newfangled machines than the drivers who fitfully handled them. The modern, uniform system of red, yellow, and green traffic signals is the outgrowth of a traffic lamp invented to sort out these early-twentieth-century problems. The year was 1912, and the inventor was Lester Farnsworth Wire, head of the Salt Lake City police department's traffic squad. Kevin Bechstrom, in a salute to this forgotten benefactor, says that Wire got the idea for a traffic light while reading the Bible—the part in the Sermon on the Mount about not hiding your candle under a bushel, but putting it on a candlestick instead (Matt. 5:15). For his candlestick Wire chose a ten-foot pole, and for his candles he used two Mazda lamps, painted red for stop and green for go. He set up the contraption at Main and Second, where it gathered gawkers for a while but was eventually accepted as good sense.

Wire's model had only a red and a green light, for stop and start, and in the 1920s many cities stayed with that simple design: it was familiar to many people from the red and green lights of seagoing vessels, and from railroad signals. Today's yellow, or amber, light was introduced later, and for some time it met with opposition. Seems that drivers approaching a yellow signal, rather than slowing down as they should, floored the accelerator instead. They called it amber-rushing then.

DRIVING ON THE RIGHT

Until about two hundred years ago, travelers approaching each other on the same road would typically veer to the left. This custom made logical sense given the right-dominance of most human beings and the perilous nature of travel: Whether you were on a horse or afoot, you would want to keep your weapon arm as near as possible to the approaching stranger, in case he proved to be up to no good. According to Richard Hopper, the left-passing custom was made official in the year 1300, by Pope Boniface VIII, who to prevent snarling among pilgrims in that Jubilee Year, proclaimed that all those coming to Rome should keep to the left of the road. The edict, Hopper claims, "had something of the force of law in much of western Europe for over 500 years." In Great Britain and in nations influenced by her, although the edict has long been forgotten, the custom still has the force of law.

In America the custom and the law are reversed. Albert Rose suggests that "a smoldering opposition to customs of the Old World" may have contributed to the switch, and that in wild-and-woolly America it made sense to keep to the right because one's rifle, cradled in the crook of the left arm, could then cover the stranger in case of trouble. These are plausible secondary reasons. The primary reason for the American right-hand rule, as both Rose and Hopper acknowledge, has to do with the construction of freight wagons, particularly the Conestoga "prairie schooners" that carried so many settlers west. Few of these wagons had front seats, and the driver would control a four-horse or four-oxen team while sitting on the left rear animal. The left was preferred to the right because that position provided marginally greater efficiency in whip-handling for a right-handed driver. Two vehicles driven in this fashion would logically veer right when approaching, so their drivers could have a clear view of their wagons' closely passing wheel hubs. The custom was first made law in 1792, by a Pennsylvania statute governing turnpike travel. When automobiles came in a century later, the placement of the steering wheel reflected the position of the early Conestoga drivers.

French freight wagons, Hopper points out, were similar in construction to American ones, and so the right-passing rule came in there, too—helped along, possibly, by Jacobin resistance to taking orders from a medieval Italian. British freight wagons, on the other hand, had a driver's seat in front of the load, and British wagon drivers, possibly in order to avoid entangling their whips in their cargo, sat on the right side of the seat. British steering wheels reflect this position, and British drivers, as Boniface intended, pass to this day on the left.

MOUNTING HORSES FROM THE LEFT

In Roy Rogers movies of the 1940s, Roy occasionally mounted Trigger leapfrog style, from the rear. This was arresting not only because of the showmanship, but because it was so anomalous: As any novice equestrian will tell you, you always mount your horse from the side, and that side is always the left.

The left-side-only tradition has nothing to do with the structure or neurophysiology of the animal. Centuries ago, when many riders carried swords, they carried them on their left hips, for easier access with the right hand. Mounting a horse from the left was the most efficient way of getting on the animal without the weapon getting in your way. In time the left-side mount became de rigueur, whether or not you had a sword. Our local equestrian authority tells me that tradition dictates not only mounting styles, but virtually everything in the horse world. One curries, bridles, and saddles in a time-honored, prescribed pattern not because the animal has been trained to expect it, and will bite or buck if you ignore it, but because it's "the way things are done." Few horses, evidently, are so neurotic that they will balk at being mounted from the right.

BAKER'S DOZEN

In the sixteenth century, English bakers could be fined heavily for selling short-weighted loaves of bread, and to guard against this possibility it became customary for them to throw in an extra loaf, called the "in bread," whenever a retailer purchased a dozen. Thus a dozen plus one became known as a baker's dozen—a rare instance in which the number 13 has a positive connotation.

The phrase, like the practice, is more common in England than in America. Eric Partridge gives three interesting variations. In rhyming slang, *baker's dozen* stands for *cousin*. In the mid-nineteenth century, Baker's Dozen was the nickname for the British army's Thirteenth Hussars regiment. And in colloquial speech, to give someone a baker's dozen is to thrash him vigorously—laying on a full complement of blows, plus one.

RED–LETTER DAYS

A red-letter day, indicating a day of special importance or good fortune, was originally a Sunday, a saint's day, or any other feast day in the Christian calendar. In the Church of England, the distinction was more precise: Red-letter days were those feast days for which the Book of Common Prayer had stipulated a collect, gospel, and epistle. The name arose because in hand-lettered medieval calendars, prayer books, and almanacs, monks articulated the names of feast days in red ink; all other days in the calendar, because of their less-colorful inking, were known as black-letter days.

STRIPED BARBER POLES

In the Middle Ages, hair was not the only thing that barbers cut. They also performed surgery, tooth extraction, and bloodletting. French authorities drew a fine distinction between academic surgeons (surgeons of the long robe) and barber surgeons (surgeons of the short robe), but the latter were sufficiently accepted by the fourteenth century to have their own guild, and in 1505 they were admitted to the faculty of the University of Paris. As an indication of their medical importance, Harry Perelman points out that Ambroise Pare, "the father of modern surgery and the greatest surgeon of the Renaissance," began as a barber surgeon.

The barber pole as a symbol of the profession is a legacy of bloodletting. The barber surgeon's necessities for that curious custom were a staff for the patient to grasp (so the veins on the arm would stand out sharply), a basin to hold leeches and catch blood, and a copious supply of linen bandages. After the operation was completed, the bandages would be hung on the staff and sometimes placed outside as advertisement. Twirled by the wind, they would form a red-and-white spiral pattern that was later adopted for painted poles. The earliest poles were surmounted by a leech basin, which in time was transformed into a ball.

What about the blue stripe? Esoteric researchers suggest that red, blue, and white stood originally for arterial blood, venous blood, and clean linen. Others say that red and blue were the colors enjoined, respectively, on academic and barber surgeons under England's King Henry VIII. It's also likely that American patriotism played a part, since according to barber pole manufacturer William Marvey, the blue stripe was introduced in this country, and not until the turn of the century.

BLUE RIBBON

The association of high achievement with the color blue is fairly widespread in the West. The blue ribbon is given for first place in most sporting events, and many decorations of Western nations feature blue very prominently—for example, the French Order of Merit, the Vatican's Order of Pius, and the American Congressional Medal of Honor, Distinguished Service Cross, and Navy Cross. The association probably originated in England in 1348, when King Edward III chose a broad dark-blue ribbon as the badge of his newly formed Order of the Garter. Behind his choice, as Rudolph Brasch speculates, may have been the awe that human beings feel for the sky.

BIBLIOGRAPHY

The standard reference works most helpful to me were the *Oxford English Dictionary (OED);* Eric Partridge's *Dictionary of Slang and Unconventional English* (8th ed. by Paul Beale, 1984); Mitford Mathews's *Dictionary of Americanisms on Historical Principles* (1956); Harold Wentworth and Stuart Berg Flexner's *Pocket Dictionary of American Slang* (1969); the *New Catholic Encyclopedia* (1967); the *Encyclopaedia Judaica* (1971); the multivolume *Encyclopedia of Religion and Ethics* (under the general editorship of James Hastings, 1908–1927); and the Funk & Wagnalls *Standard Dictionary of Folklore, Mythology, and Legend* (edited by Maria Leach, 1950). I am also grateful to the authors of the following specialized sources:

Allen, E. John B., "Winter Culture," *Journal of American Culture,* vol. 6, no. 1 (Spring 1983).

Baring-Gould, Sabine, *Strange Survivals,* Methuen, 1892.

Barker, Lewis, ed., *The Psychobiology of Human Food Selection,* Avi, 1982.

Barnett, James H., *The American Christmas,* Macmillan, 1954.

Bates, Marston, *Gluttons and Libertines,* Vintage, 1971.

Benedict, Ruth, *Patterns of Culture,* Houghton Mifflin, 1959 (1934).

Benthall, Jonathan, and Ted Polhemus, eds., *The Body as a Means of Expression,* Dutton, 1975.

Bechstrom, Kevin, "A Salute to Lester Farnsworth Wire," *AASHTO Quarterly,* April 1986.

Birdwhistell, Ray L., *Kinesics and Context,* University of Pennsylvania Press, 1970.

Blakey, George G., *The Diamond,* Paddington Press, 1977.

Booth, David A., "How Nutritional Effects of Foods Can Influence People's Dietary Choices," in Barker.

Bossard, James H. S., and Eleanor S. Boll, *Ritual in Family Living,* University of Pennsylvania Press, 1950.

Bourne, Henry, *Antiquitates Vulgares,* J. White, 1725.

Bowman, Leroy, *The American Funeral,* Public Affairs Press, 1959.

Brasch, Rudolph, *How Did It Begin?* Longmans, 1965.

Brewer, E. Cobham, *Brewer's Dictionary of Phrase and Fable,* ed. by Ivor Evans, Harper & Row, 1981 (1870).

Brod, I. Jack, with Tad Tuleja, *Consumer's Guide to Buying and Selling Gold, Silver, and Diamonds,* Doubleday, 1985.

Carroll, Michael P. "The Logic of Anglo-American Meals," *Journal of American Culture,* vol. 5, no. 3 (Fall 1982).

Cavan, Sherri, *Liquor License: An Ethnography of Bar Behavior,* Aldine, 1966.

Cirlot, J. E., *A Dictionary of Symbols,* trans. by Jack Sage, Philosophical Library, 1981.

Cox, Harvey, *The Feast of Fools,* Harper & Row, 1970.

Craven, Gerald, and Richard Moseley, "Actors on the Canvas Stage: The Dramatic Conventions of Professional Wrestling," *Journal of Popular Culture,* vol. 6, no. 2 (Fall 1972).

Crawley, Ernest, *The Mystic Rose,* rev. ed. by Theodore Besterman, Meridian Books, 1960 (1927).

Crippen, T. G., *Christmas and Christmas Lore,* Gale Research, 1971 (1923).

Darwin, Charles, *The Expression of the Emotions in Man and Animals,* University of Chicago Press, 1965 (1872).

Delind, Laura B., "Bingo," *Journal of Popular Culture,* vol. 18, no. 2 (Fall 1984).

Dickson, Paul, *The Great American Ice Cream Book,* Galahad Books, 1972.

Dundes, Alan, "Chain Letter," *Northwest Folklore,* vol. 1, no. 2 (1966).

———, "Here I Sit," *Papers of the Kroeber Anthropological Society,* vol. 34 (1966).

Eames, Edwin, and Howard Robboy, "The Socio-Cultural Context of an Italian-American Dietary Item," in Jorgensen and Truzzi.

Edmunds, Lowell, *The Silver Bullet,* Greenwood Press, 1981.

Eibl-Eibesfeldt, Irenäus, "Similarities and Differences Between Cultures in Expressive Movements," in Hinde (1975).

Eichler, Lillian, *The Customs of Mankind,* Doubleday, Doran, 1924.

———, *Today's Etiquette,* New Home Library, 1943 (1924).

Eliade, Mircea, *Cosmos and History: The Myth of the Eternal Return,* trans. by Willard Trask, Harper, 1959.

Elias, Norbert, *The Civilizing Process,* trans. by Edmund Jephcott, Urizen Books, 1978 (1939).

Ellis, Havelock, "The Origins of the Kiss," in *Studies in the Psychology of Sex,* Random House, 1936.

Elworthy, Frederick, *Horns of Honour,* John Murray, 1900.

Farb, Peter, and George Armelagos, *Consuming Passions,* Houghton Mifflin, 1980.

Fenton, Alexander, and Trefor Owen, eds., *Food in Perspective,* John Donald, 1981.

Fielding, William J., *Strange Customs of Courtship and Marriage*, Circle Books, 1942.

Firth, Raymond, "Postures and Gestures of Respect," in Polhemus.

Flügel, J. C., *The Psychology of Clothes*, Hogarth Press, 1950.

Ford, Clellan S., and Frank A. Beach, *Patterns of Sexual Behavior*, Harper & Brothers, 1951.

Fossel, Peter V., "Hex Signs: Chust for Nice," *Americana*, July–August 1982.

Frazer, Sir James George, *The Golden Bough*, Macmillan, 1951.

Gelman, Eric, with John McCormick and Carolyn Friday, "Let's Not Have Lunch," *Business Week*, June 30, 1986.

Goethals, Gregor T., *The TV Ritual*, Beacon Press, 1981.

Goffman, Erving, *Asylums*, Doubleday, 1961.

———, *Behavior in Public Places*, Free Press, 1963.

Guthrie, R. Dale, *Body Hot Spots*, Van Nostrand Reinhold, 1976.

Habenstein, Robert, and William Lamers, *The History of American Funeral Directing*, Bulfin Printers, 1955.

Harmer, Ruth, *The High Cost of Dying*, Crowell-Collier, 1963.

Harris, Marvin, *Good to Eat*, Simon & Schuster, 1985.

Hawes, Elizabeth, *It's Still Spinach*, Little, Brown, 1954.

Hendley, W. Clark, "Dear Abby, Miss Lonelyhearts, and the Eighteenth Century," *Journal of Popular Culture*, vol. 11, no. 2 (Fall 1977).

Hertz, Robert, "The Pre-Eminence of the Right Hand," (1909), trans. by Rodney Needham, in Needham.

Hinde, R. A., ed., *Non-Verbal Communication*, Cambridge University Press, 1975.

Hite, Shere, *The Hite Report*, Dell, 1978.

Hopper, Richard H., "Left-Right," *Transportation Quarterly*, vol. 36, no. 4 (October 1982).

Hughes, Pennethorne, *Witchcraft*, Penguin Books, 1967.

Huntington, Richard, and Peter Metcalf, *Celebrations of Death*, Cambridge University Press, 1979.

Hyde, Lewis, *The Gift*, Random House, 1983.

Iversen, William, *O the Times! O the Manners!* William Morrow, 1965.

Jerome, Norge W., "Frozen (TV) Dinners," in Fenton and Owen.

Johnson, Clyde Sanfred, *Fraternities in Our Colleges*, National Interfraternity Foundation, 1972.

Jorgensen, Joseph G., and Marcello Truzzi, eds., *Anthropology in American Life*, Prentice-Hall, 1974.

King, W. S., "Hand Gestures," *Western Folklore*, vol. 8 (1949).

Kinsey, Alfred, Wardell Pomeroy, and Clyde Martin, *Sexual Behavior in the Human Male*, Saunders, 1948.

Kinsey, Alfred, Wardell Pomeroy, Clyde Martin, and Paul Gebhard, *Sexual Behavior in the Human Female,* W. B. Saunders, 1953.

Knowlson, T. Sharper, *The Origins of Popular Superstitions and Customs,* J. Pott, n.d.

Koch, Rudolph, *The Book of Signs,* Dover, 1955 (1930).

Kottak, Conrad P., "Anthropological Analysis of Mass Enculturation," in C. P. Kottak, ed., *Researching American Culture,* University of Michigan Press, 1982.

——, "Ritual at McDonald's," *Natural History,* vol. 87, no. 1 (1978).

Krythe, Maymie R., *All About American Holidays,* Harper & Row, 1962.

——, *All About Christmas,* Harper & Brothers, 1954.

Lamm, Maurice, *The Jewish Way in Love and Marriage,* Harper & Row, 1980.

Lawrence, Robert Means, *The Magic of the Horse-Shoe,* Singing Tree Press, 1968 (1898).

Leach, Maria, *God Had a Dog,* Rutgers University Press, 1961.

——, *The Soup Stone,* Funk & Wagnalls, 1954.

Lewis, Linda Rannells, *Birthdays,* Atlantic–Little, Brown, 1976.

Linton, Ralph, and Adelin Linton, *Halloween Through Twenty Centuries,* Henry Schuman, 1950.

Lovette, Leland P., *Naval Customs,* U.S. Naval Institute, 1939.

McCarthy, Joe, "The Gra-a-nd Parade," *American Heritage,* vol. 20, no. 2 (February 1969).

MacCulloch, J. A., "Baptism (Ethnic)," in *Encyclopedia of Religion and Ethics.*

MacRae, Donald G., "The Body and Social Metaphor," in Benthall and Polhemus.

Malinowski, Bronislaw, *The Sexual Life of Savages in North-Western Melanesia,* Harcourt, Brace, 1929.

Mariani, John F., *The Dictionary of American Food and Drink,* Ticknor & Fields, 1983.

Martin, Judith, *Common Courtesy,* Atheneum, 1985.

——, *Miss Manners' Guide to Excruciatingly Correct Behavior,* Atheneum, 1982.

Miner, Horace, "Body Ritual Among the Nacirema" (1956), in Polhemus.

Mintz, Sidney W., "Choice and Occasion," in Barker.

Mitford, Jessica, *The American Way of Death,* Simon & Schuster, 1963.

Monahan, Barbara, *A Dictionary of Russian Gesture,* Hermitage, 1983.

Morris, Desmond, *Bodywatching,* Equinox, 1985.

——, *The Naked Ape,* Dell, 1969.

——, Peter Collett, Peter Marsh, and Marie O'Shaughnessy, *Gestures,* Stein & Day, 1979.

Moskowitz, Milton, Michael Katz, and Robert Levering, *Everybody's Business,* Harper & Row, 1980.

Myers, Robert J., *Celebrations,* Doubleday, 1972.

Needham, Rodney, ed., *Right and Left,* University of Chicago Press, 1973.

Parry, Albert, *Tattoo,* Simon & Schuster, 1933.

Perella, Nicolas James, *The Kiss Sacred and Profane,* University of California Press, 1969.

Perelman, Harry, "The Barber Pole," *Lynx Eye* (Westside Hospital, Los Angeles), May 1974.

Perutz, Kathrin, *Beyond the Looking Glass,* William Morrow, 1970.

Pike, E. Royston, *Love in Ancient Rome,* Frederick Muller, 1965.

———, *The Strange Ways of Man,* Hart, 1966.

Polhemus, Ted, ed., *The Body Reader,* Pantheon Books, 1978.

Post, Emily, *Etiquette,* Funk & Wagnalls, 1952 (1922).

Radcliffe-Brown, A. R., *The Andaman Islanders,* Cambridge University Press, 1933.

Radford, E., and M.A. Radford, *Encyclopedia of Superstitions,* rev. ed. by Christina Hole, Hutchinson, 1975.

Ramsey, Richard David, "The People Versus Smokey Bear," *Journal of Popular Culture,* vol. 13, no. 2 (Fall 1979).

Rashdall, Hastings, *The Universities of Europe in the Middle Ages,* ed. by F. M. Powicke and A. B. Emden, Oxford, 1969 (1936).

Read, Allen Walker, *Classic American Graffiti,* Maledicta Press, 1977 (1935).

———, "The Spelling Bee," *PMLA,* vol. 56 (1941).

Renner, H. D., *The Origin of Food Habits,* Faber & Faber, 1944.

Romberg, Rosemary, *Circumcision,* Bergin & Garvey, 1985.

Root, Waverley, and Richard de Rochemont, *Eating in America,* Ecco Press, 1981.

Rose, Albert Chatelier, *Public Roads of the Past,* American Association of State Highway Officials, 1952.

Ross, Elizabeth, "Patty Smith Hill," in *Dictionary of American Biography,* Supplement 4, Scribner's, 1974.

Ross, Eric B., "Patterns of Diet and Forces of Production," in E. B. Ross, *Beyond the Myths of Culture,* Academic, 1980.

Rozin, Elisabeth, "The Structure of Cuisine," in Barker.

Rucker, Ellie, "Buttons Placed for Swords, Kids," in *American-Statesman* (Austin), July 13, 1986.

Rudofsky, Bernard, *The Unfashionable Human Body,* Doubleday, 1971.

Samtur, Susan, with Tad Tuleja, *Cashing in at the Checkout,* Stonesong Press, 1979.

Schein, John, Edwin Jablonski, and Barbara Wohlfahrt, *The Art of Tipping,* Sun Press, 1984.

Schlesinger, Arthur M., *Learning How to Behave,* Macmillan, 1946.

Scott, John Findley, "The American College Sorority," *American Sociological Review,* vol. 30, no. 4 (August 1965).

Scutt, R. W. B., and Christopher Gotch, *Art, Sex and Symbol,* Barnes, 1974.

Seligson, Marcia, *The Eternal Bliss Machine,* William Morrow, 1973.

Seymour, Harold, *Baseball,* Oxford, 1960.

Sheldon, Henry D., *Student Life and Customs,* Arno Press and The New York Times, 1969 (1901).

Sherwood, Mrs. John, *Manners and Social Usages,* Harper & Brothers, 1887.

Simoons, Frederick J., *Eat Not This Flesh,* University of Wisconsin Press, 1961.

Smith, W. John, Julia Chase, and Anna Katz Lieblich, "Tongue Showing," *Semiotica,* vol. 11, no. 3 (1974).

Smith, Whitney, "Symbols of Peace and Pacifism," *Flag Bulletin,* vol. 20, no. 1 (January–February 1981).

Snyder, Phillip V., *The Christmas Tree Book,* Viking, 1976.

Staff, Frank, *The Valentine and Its Origins,* Praeger, 1969.

Starr, Michael E., "The Marlboro Man," *Journal of Popular Culture,* vol. 17, no. 4 (Spring 1984).

Stimpson, George, *A Book About a Thousand Things,* Harper & Brothers, 1946.

——, *Information Roundup,* Harper & Brothers, 1948.

Sutton-Smith, Brian, *The Folkgames of Children,* University of Texas Press, 1972.

Szasz, Kathleen, *Petishism,* Rinehart & Winston, 1969.

Taft, Philip, *The A. F. of L. in the Time of Gompers,* Harper & Brothers, 1957.

Tarshis, Barry, *The "Average American" Book,* Signet, 1981.

Thorndike, Lynn, *University Records and Life in the Middle Ages,* Octagon Books, 1971.

Tober, Barbara, *The Bride,* Abrams, 1984.

Trager, James, *The Foodbook,* Grossman, 1970.

Vanderbilt, Amy, *New Complete Book of Etiquette,* Doubleday, 1967.

Van Gennep, Arnold, *The Rites of Passage,* trans. by Monika Vizedom and Gabrielle Caffee, University of Chicago Press, 1966 (1908).

Wagner, Leopold, *Manners, Customs, and Observances,* Gale Research, 1968 (1894).

Waits, William Burnell, Jr., "The Many-Faced Custom," unpublished dissertation, Rutgers University, 1978.

Walsh, William S., *Curiosities of Popular Customs,* Gale Research, 1966 (1898).

Waterman, Philip F., *The Story of Superstition,* AMS Press, 1974 (1929).

Watts, Alan, *Easter,* Henry Schuman, 1950.

Weiser, Francis X., *The Christmas Book,* Harcourt, Brace, 1952.

————, *The Easter Book,* Harcourt, Brace, 1954.

Wellington, Raymond, "Wine in Restaurants," in Zraly.

Westermarck, Edward, *A Short History of Marriage,* Macmillan, 1930.

Wilcox, R. Turner, *Five Centuries of American Costume,* Scribner's, 1962.

Wolff, Edwin Daniel, *Why We Do It,* Books for Libraries Press, 1968 (1929).

Wynne, Peter, *Apples,* Hawthorn Books, 1975.

Zach, Paul, ed., *Florida,* Apa Productions, 1982.

Zraly, Kevin, *Windows on the World Complete Wine Course,* Sterling, 1985.